## Advance Praise for *Reclaim*

D0979494

"If you want to understand the rising preemir[...] modern-day sociopolitical landscape, you would be smart to start with Feminista Jones, a black woman writing and working at the forefront of our movements."

—IJEOMA OLUO, author of the *New York Times* bestseller
*So You Want to Talk About Race*

"*Reclaiming Our Space* is an invaluable contribution to long-overdue conversations about race, gender, and intersectionality in America. Feminista Jones combines empathy and wisdom with intellectual rigor and historical analysis to explain clearly and compellingly the central role that Black feminists play in the fight for democracy and social justice."

—SORAYA CHEMALY, director of the Women's Media Center
Speech Project and author of *Rage Becomes Her*

"*Reclaiming Our Space* is a refreshing affirmation of Black women, centering our societal roles in a way I have never read before. For those of us whose race and gender exist at a precarious intersection, *Reclaiming Our Space* is a godsend that will inform not only how we are approached and regarded by others through social media platforms but how we interact with each other and value ourselves."

—CASHAWN THOMPSON, creator of #BlackGirlMagic

"It's impossible to overstate the cultural impact of Feminista Jones. As a bold and candid voice in the blogosphere and on social media, before 'intersectional feminism' made its necessary move from the realm of academia to circulation in popular culture, Feminista spoke loudly and clearly about the particular identities and predicaments of Black women in America. She has been tough, she has been honest, and she has been that thing that ignorant people like to pretend is somehow incompatible with feminism: she's been funny. From motherhood to street harassment, she has worked to uplift issues facing Black women, time and time again, with ferocity and love."

—EVE L. EWING, author of *Electric Arches and Ghosts in the Schoolyard*

"As often as I find myself disillusioned by today's political climate, Feminista Jones reminds us that Black women have always been and continue to be at the forefront of social change both online and IRL. *Reclaiming Our Space* is a thorough and accessible history of Black feminism that reflects on our past as a means of encouraging us to move toward a better future."

—FRANCHESCA RAMSEY, host of MTV's *Decoded* and author of
*Well, That Escalated Quickly: Memoirs and Mistakes of an Accidental Activist*

"In a world where many call themselves 'feminist,' educator, healer, and community leader Feminista Jones provides tangible steps for those seeking to do a better job of showing up and holding space for Black women. *Reclaiming Our Space* is required reading for brothers who fashion themselves supporters of our sisters, as well as those who don't yet know they need to be. It's also soul food for the rest of y'all desiring to move toward a better future."

—DAVID JOHNS, executive director of the
National Black Justice Coalition

# RECLAIMING OUR SPACE

OTHER BOOKS BY FEMINISTA JONES

*The Secret of Sugar Water*

*Push the Button*

# RECLAIMING OUR SPACE

## HOW BLACK FEMINISTS ARE CHANGING THE WORLD FROM THE TWEETS TO THE STREETS

## FEMINISTA JONES

Beacon Press ■ Boston

Beacon Press
Boston, Massachusetts
www.beacon.org

Beacon Press books
are published under the auspices of
the Unitarian Universalist Association of Congregations.

22 21 20 19     8 7 6 5 4 3 2 1

This book is printed on acid-free paper that meets the uncoated paper
ANSI/NISO specifications for permanence as revised in 1992.

Text design and composition by Kim Arney

*Library of Congress Cataloging-in-Publication Data*

Names: Jones, Feminista, author.
Title: Reclaiming our space : how black feminists are changing the
world from the tweets to the streets / Feminista Jones.
Description: Boston : Beacon Press, 2019. | Includes bibliographical references.
Identifiers: LCCN 2018038259 (print) | LCCN 2018053391 (ebook) |
ISBN 9780807055380 (ebook) | ISBN 9780807055373 (paperback)
Subjects: LCSH: Womanism—United States. | Intersectionality—United States. |
Online social networks—United States. | BISAC: SOCIAL SCIENCE / Ethnic
Studies / African American Studies. | SOCIAL SCIENCE / Feminism & Feminist
Theory. | SOCIAL SCIENCE / Media Studies.
Classification: LCC HQ1197 (ebook) | LCC HQ1197 .J66 2019 (print) |
DDC 305.48/896073—dc23
LC record available at https://lccn.loc.gov/2018038259

*Dedicated to every Black girl around the world . . .*
*Freedom is coming.*

# CONTENTS

# It All Started When . . .

*I think the people who have problems with me are those who can't accept the realness of life. And if you can't accept that, then you haven't gone through what I've gone through, and if you haven't gone through it, then you can't judge me. If you don't know where I've been, then how do you know who I am.*

—LIL' KIM, game-changing hip-hop MC[2]

**T**HE FIRST TIME SOMEONE accused me of being a CIA agent, I laughed. Hard. I could not believe that anyone would make such an absurd assertion. Me? I'm just one woman, born in Queens and raised in the Bronx, a hood girl made good, putting a big, fancy degree to work and action by fighting systemic racism, sexism, and classism. I have been a pro–Black liberation activist, feminist writer, and community organizer since the late 1990s. Yet somehow my public identity as a feminist woman led to suspicions that I was a government agent. This was a disturbing revelation to me, to say the least.

Then someone accused me of being an FBI agent charged with imprisoning Black men in an effort to further destroy the Black family. This time I did not laugh as hard. Instead, I began to experience a heavy burden of hopelessness and futility. How could people whom I have gone out of my way to defend and for whose needs I have advocated—at a risk to my own safety and that of my family—believe I would do anything to break up Black families or damage Black communities? I began to wonder seriously: Who and what am I fighting for?

When I was growing up in the 1980s and 1990s, New York City was experiencing unprecedented socioeconomic and political upheaval. The aftermath of the Vietnam War left families torn apart and many Black men unemployed. In 1971, the unemployment rate for Black male Vietnam War veterans under age twenty-four was 20.9 percent, compared with 17.4 percent for Black nonveterans under twenty-four, and 14.6 percent for veterans under twenty-four as a whole.[3] The crack epidemic of the 1980s swept through inner cities. Political corruption was at an all-time high. Disparities between the haves and have-nots were tremendous. To be poor in New York City at this time meant being susceptible to violent crime, inadequate education, food insecurity, and more.[4] My parents—married when I was four years old, divorced by the time I was six—worked, but our family was low-income, and we relied on housing subsidies and public assistance to make ends meet. After my parents divorced, my mom and I moved around a lot before settling into life in the Bronx, hands down the greatest borough of New York City but also the poorest—over 50 percent of Bronx neighborhoods have high or extreme poverty rates.[5] The Bronx is also the birthplace of hip-hop culture, and it was there and during the golden age of hip-hop that I began to figure out who I was, who I wanted to be, and what I wanted to do with my life.

My mother, a lesbian womanist and early AIDS activist, did everything she could to make sure I had access to the best education possible, regardless of cost. I became a "prep school Negro"—one of the young "gifted and talented" poor kids from the inner city who got a shot at obtaining a privileged education at one of America's elite boarding schools.[6] I went on to the Ivy League for college and then received advanced degrees and certifications. But my first exposure to feminist thought was not in the classroom. It was by way of female MCs in the late 1980s and early 1990s. I did not recognize it at the time (having no point of reference for contextualizing their messages), but they were the earliest influences in the development of my feminist identity.

When I first heard "Ladies First" by Queen Latifah and "Shake Your Thang" by Salt-N-Pepa, I was more excited about their songs than I was about any other hip-hop music. And when TLC debuted with *Oooooohhh . . . On the TLC Tip*, I grew more and more excited about being a girl. A few years later in boarding school, in English classes that focused on women writers and feminist literature, I was exposed to academic feminist thought. Though I was only sixteen at the time, the simple idea that women deserve equal access to social, economic, and political resources and opportunities resonated deeply within me. I grew up in neighborhoods where women were incredibly strong, but my exposure was limited to the experiences of lower-income women and single mothers. Reading about women who were different from me made me feel connected. Though my teachers made genuine attempts to diversify content, with sprinkles of Alice Walker and Maxine Hong Kingston, most of the authors we read were White women. After writing my first critical essays and literary analysis about Sylvia Plath and Virginia Woolf, I decided feminism was where my heart was at, and I became determined to explore more feminist theory *and* seek out more women of color authors.

In college, the game changed. There, I had plenty of access to a wide range of feminist thinkers, writers, and activists, and not just via books. My professors, the visiting guests we hosted, and occasional lecturers like Angela Davis and bell hooks, were all within reach—literally. It was then that I centered my education on Black studies and the sociology of deviance and law, with women's studies thrown into the mix. I realized at age nineteen that I was, in fact, a Black feminist woman, and I began to embrace that identity proudly and let it guide my words and eventual work as a social work administrator, writer, and activist.

Today, as Feminista Jones™, a name I chose for myself as a writer in 2011 (in homage to Cleopatra Jones, the no-nonsense Blaxploitation-era character made popular by actress Tamara Dobson), I focus my writing on various aspects of Black cultural identities, with a specific focus on Black womanhood. I am a "social justice warrior," as those who oppose freedom and equality for all tend to refer to those of us who fight against systemic oppression. I'm a vocal advocate for Black girls and women, and I use my platforms to encourage challenging discourse, inspire and motivate people into action, and amplify the narratives that often go ignored by the mainstream media, which usually center Whiteness and White experiences.

My identity and work are not always embraced by or accepted among my peers, however. Among some segments of the Black community, there is a commonly held belief that Black women who identify as feminist are not truly focused on the liberation and social, economic, and political equality of Black people. Instead, they believe we are working to destroy the community by turning Black women and men against each other. They do not believe Black women need any special focus when it comes to liberation—that our issues are simply Black issues, and that when Black people achieve liberation, Black women, too, will be included in whatever we sow from our freedom fighting. These segments believe Black feminist women are "divisive," and that we do the work of White supremacy by distracting people from the *real* issues.

I'm not the only feminist these detractors claim is working with the United States government. Gloria Steinem has been accused of being a CIA plant who's lured Black women into embracing feminism in a larger plot to make Black communities implode and self-destruct.[7] Other times, they say we are working with groups like COINTELPRO, the FBI's counterintelligence program that operated from 1956 to 1971 to diffuse Communist Party activities, causing chaos and division. They simply do not believe that Black Feminism is a legitimate liberation movement, and they have convinced themselves that any Black woman who subscribes to Black feminist theoretical frameworks and ideologies is a White man–worshipping, self-loathing, traitorous agent of White supremacy.

Well, I'm none of those things.

I am a proud queer Black feminist woman. My Black feminist identity has been influenced and shaped by the works of Sojourner Truth, Audre Lorde, Queen Latifah, Angela Davis, Alice Walker, Lisa "Left Eye" Lopes, Florynce Kennedy, Missy Elliott, Michele Wallace, Patricia Hill Collins, Amy Garvey, @TheTrudz, Kimberlé Crenshaw, and the Combahee River Collective, among many others. My work to upend misconceptions and to educate others follows in this long tradition. The Combahee River Collective has been especially crucial in influencing the work of today's Black feminists, whether younger feminists or those newer to feminist theory recognize the group's name or not. The collective met several times at retreats in the late 1970s to discuss the state of Black Feminism and how Black women could and should move forward. Chirlane McCray, the First Lady of New York City and wife of Mayor Bill DeBlasio, and the acclaimed writer and activist Audre Lorde were members. At that time, the collective saw themselves as "modern" feminists in the tradition of their foremothers Ida B. Wells, Mary Church Terrell, and Sojourner Truth. In *The Combahee River Collective Statement*, an official manifesto authored primarily by activists Barbara Smith, Beverly Smith, and Demita Frazier, the women offered that they were "particularly committed to working on those struggles in which race, sex, and class are simultaneous factors in oppression."[8]

What made their work incredibly important is the consideration they took to become more inclusive of intersectional identities and the experiences of Black women throughout the African diaspora; so-called Third World experiences with poverty and maternal health were priorities for the collective. They were invested in the dismantling of patriarchy and capitalism, which they believed were the greatest impediments to women's liberation. "We realize that the only people who care enough about us to work consistently for our liberation is us"—this was a bold assertion that Black women could rely neither on Black men nor on White women to assist them in their fight to be regarded as human beings with full rights and deserving of dignity and respect and the right to pursue liberty and happiness, as was promised to all Americans. We see echoes of that today, in the reluctant acceptance of the "We all we got" refrain, frequently used by Black feminist women in online spaces. Sometimes, we truly feel that we are all we have. This has increased the importance and impact of digital spaces not only as a tool for activists but as a place to be heard and supported.[9]

Go to almost any social media platform today and you will see a gathering of some of the most important feminist thinkers of modern generations—Generation X women who grew up jumping double Dutch and scanning card catalogs at local libraries are building communities with millennial women who grew up with caller ID and Google in their pockets. Who could have imagined that the pound sign, once valuable primarily for its use on touch-tone landline phones, would become one of the most powerful weapons for Black feminists? Who could have predicted that people who never set foot on a college campus, much less in a specialized journalism school, would have international audiences reading their cultural and sociopolitical analyses? Or have their work be part of a rigorous academic curriculum at universities they could never afford to attend? That is what Black feminist activism looks like today.

Black feminist women are being heard in ways they have never been heard before. Social media networks provide platforms for conversations that we have long been having in our hair salons and our churches, by our watercoolers and in our breakrooms, and in our housing project courtyards and systematically segregated classrooms. What was once whispered or only shared in the sacred comforts of sister circles and ladies' brunches is now on public display for all to access, learn from, and build upon. The ways in which knowledge is created and shared has transformed in large part due to the explosion of digital media, and Black women have been trailblazers in this new digital landscape. We have to look at how, over the last decade, Black women have harnessed their ingenuity and their magic and have taken to digital platforms to advance the fight toward liberation while honoring the ways in which Black Feminism has been the guiding theoretical framework for our collective progress.

I recognize that while Black people experience the perils of systemic racism, Black women are further subjected to misogyny, and Black queer people to queerphobia. Not to accept this is to do harm. There is no liberation for Black people without complete liberation for *all* Black people in *all* ways, without exception.

I believe in the radical notion that Black liberation must center the experiences of Black women, Black LGBTQ people, Black people living in poverty, Black disabled people, and other Black people who remain marginalized even within our collectively marginalized community. The "trickle down" approach to Black liberation in which Black cisgender, heterosexual men are centered and exalted as leaders who are first in line to be free is as effective an approach as Reaganomics; without focused work to eradicate the insidious permeation of these oppressions, we will only get as far as our internalized hatred permits. Our children and grand-children deserve better.

So how do we move forward? What do we all lose by *not* moving forward? What does "moving forward" even look like? And what innovations and political and societal progress is stymied in our refusal to deal with all this?

Let's find out.

# CHAPTER 1

# #BlackFeminism 101

**B**LACK FEMINISM IS THE key to Black liberation. I believe this without quiver or qualm, as I have yet to encounter any other theoretical template that offers a better pathway to the promise of Black people's liberation from centuries of systemic race-based oppression. Everything represented within and by the Black feminist movement affirms the entirety and complexity of life at the intersections of not only race and gender but also sexual identity, ethnicity, class, religion, size, (dis)ability, access, immigration status, and nationality. It maintains that sexism, racism, and classism function *together* and are not individual oppressions to be fought separately. It understands that *all* Black people must be accepted and affirmed as human beings worthy of freedom, liberty, dignity, and civil rights if *any* of us are to be. In this way, Black Feminism inherently advocates for Black men, disabled Black folks, queer Black folks, poor Black folks, illiterate Black folks, undocumented Black immigrants, fat Black folks, Black folks who pray, and Black folks who have found another way. I repeat, Black Feminism is the key to Black liberation.

Black Feminism is also hardly a new concept. It exists out of necessity, though if the feminist and Black Power movements had been fully inclusive of the unique needs and concerns of Black women, perhaps we would have found ourselves comfortably enveloped in those fights. When feminist movements for women's equality center and prioritize White women and Black movements for racial equality center and prioritize Black men, all the women are White and all the Blacks are men.[1] Black feminist women, as freedom fighters who exist at the intersection of both fights, should therefore be the accepted voices of wisdom when it comes to matters of the intersectional fight for liberation from multiple oppressions. Black Feminism also finds itself involved in efforts to push forward the rights of *all* women, taken up by respected critical thinkers and activists but mostly by women at the grassroots level, carrying the burdens of the struggle and acting as bridges for others to cross to achieve their own personal freedoms.

Over the years, I have studied the ever-developing Black feminist theoretical framework (the books, essays, speeches, and art that present and represent theories, experiences, and recommendations for liberation through a Black feminist lens), reviewing the histories of the movement beginning with Black feminists in America, then shifting my focus toward Black Feminism in Great Britain, the Caribbean, and West Africa, committing myself not only to sharing what I have learned but also connecting online and in person with Black feminist women and those who embrace Black Feminism, all around the world. What has been the most inspiring to me in all that I have learned and seen has been Black Feminism's evolution over time.

Scholar and activist Angela Davis dates Black feminist work in the Americas to the antebellum acts of resistance enacted by enslaved Black women, where their struggle was an intrinsic element in the fight for Black freedom. She writes that "by virtue of the brutal force of circumstances, the black woman was assigned the mission of promoting the consciousness and practice of resistance," and while much of Black liberation movement studies have focused on the role of Black men within the resistance, there has been "very little about the unique relationship black women bore to the resistance struggles during slavery."[2]

This notion is supported by Sojourner Truth's address to the 1867 American Equal Rights Association, in which she called attention to how her advocacy was different from White women's and Black men's:

> I suppose I am about the only colored woman who goes about to speak for the rights of the colored women. I want to keep the thing stirring, now that the ice is cracked . . . I have been in Washington about three

years, seeing about these colored people. Now colored men have the
right to vote. There ought to be equal rights now more than ever, since
colored people have got their freedom.[3]

Here, Truth exhibits support for the efforts made by both White
women for women's rights and Black men for Black people's rights, and
she positions herself as one to bring the movements together or at least
serve as an example of why Black women must be represented. In her
mind, it was rather simple—both groups deserved to be liberated from oppression, and could work together to ensure that all are afforded the rights
and liberties of free White men. As the tensions of racism and sexism
proved to be difficult to overcome (and linger still, continuing to disrupt
our lives in the twenty-first century), Truth offered the most reasonable
solution: listen to Black women.

Sojourner Truth, as well as Amy Jacques Garvey, Dorothy Height,
Mary Church Terrell, and Anna Julia Cooper are among names that *should*
immediately come to mind when thinking of the earliest Black feminist
women in the US (see Terrell's notion of the "double handicap of race and
sex"[4]). Their ideas, their work, and their experiences as freedom fighters
are clearly in line with what we understand modern Black Feminism to
be, yet there is general reluctance to label them as such. At its core, Black
Feminism is the embodiment of vital, multilayered, anti-oppression work,
born of a natural understanding of resistance-as-survival. If we want to
broaden our understanding of it fully, we cannot ignore its roots.

Take sociologist Anna Julia Cooper, whose work around the turn of
the twentieth century significantly influenced conversations about race
and gender in the academy.

Cooper identified the oppressive similarity between racism and sexism
when she made the following observation: "As our Caucasian barristers are
not to blame if they cannot *quite* put themselves in the dark man's place,
neither should the dark man be wholly expected fully and adequately to
reproduce the exact Voice of the Black Woman."[5] Cooper called out the
erasure of Black women's voices and critiqued Black men who spoke of
the "Black experience" without including a nuanced understanding of
Black female identity. Speaking of the importance of Black women leaders

to the fight for Black liberation, and the need to confront the intersection of oppressions experienced by them, Cooper asserted that "when and where I enter, in the quiet, undisputed dignity of my womanhood, without violence and without suing or special patronage, then and there the whole Negro race enters with me."[6] Cooper inserts Black Feminism into her Black liberation praxis—that is to say, her actionable steps toward the practice of Black liberation, as opposed to mulling it theoretically—when she notes the Black woman "is confronted by both a woman question and a race problem."[7]

Truth and Cooper span decades of early Black feminist work in the United States, presenting a broad spectrum of shared experiences and awareness between a formerly enslaved, illiterate woman (Truth) and an academic historian and social scientist (Cooper). I offer their contributions as examples of how Black women are uniquely qualified to comment on how Blackness and womanhood manifest and affect life outcomes. I also offer them as a counternarrative to the understanding that remains entirely too pervasive in conversations about Black Feminism's origins, purpose, and impact on the Black community. This documented history flies in the face of ahistorical fools' assertions on social media, in YouTube videos, and on the street corners of every Dr. Martin Luther King Jr. Boulevard in America that Black Feminism was created by White women to destroy Black families. There is more than enough proof of Black women's longtime embrace of feminism, even in periods when expressing support for Black women's equality posed double the safety risks. Further, since Black Feminism has consistently posed a tangible threat to Black male hegemony and White female privilege, I always deem it important to point out that Black women have been focused on the *same* issues for over a century and we are neither better nor worse on one battlefront. Where all the women are White and all the Blacks are men, we are not White enough to be women and too womanly to be Black.

Spurred by the need to adapt to societal changes, including increased access to higher education and employment, legislative advances for Black people and for women, shifts in views on marriage and childbearing, Black Feminism has gone through an interesting and necessary metamorphosis, adapting its focus to the times. Whereas bearing witness at White liberal conventions was a preferred method of activism for Truth and her peers,[8] and presenting social science research and analysis within the academy and beyond was the path of Cooper and her contemporaries,[9] the Harlem Renaissance in the 1920s found Black Feminism heavily embedded in Black women's art. We have to consider that existing as Black and women under any system of oppression allows little opportunity to alleviate the weight of one's identities, which inform nearly every experience one has navigating society. Perhaps one reason for the stereotypes of Black women's strength and endurance is the indefatigable resilience of Black women. When we think about how sistas have coped with the weight of historic oppression, we see that since the Civil War and Reconstruction, art became a popular method of processing, coping with, and expressing one's pain, as well as healing from it. The mainstream emergence of Black women's literary voices and artistic performance during the Harlem Renaissance is evidence that our fight for liberation on multiple fronts persisted.[10]

Poet Gwendolyn Bennett centered Black girl pain in "To a Dark Girl," a poignant piece speaking to the unique scars darker Black girls and women bear. Then there was Jessie Redmon Fauset, without whom it has been argued that the Harlem Renaissance would never have happened.[11] Outside of her editorial work at the NAACP's the *Crisis*, she wrote of Black social inequality in her debut novel, *There Is Confusion*, but she never achieved a high level of success and acknowledgment because she was a woman who wrote primarily about women performers like Josephine Baker, Ma Rainey, and Bessie Smith. These women *must* be noted as early sex-positive Black feminists, as their overt sexual self-expression challenged not only the standards of decorum for all women of the time but also the stringent guidance of the Black Church, and the demoralized, subjugated sexual identities of Black people postslavery. Their performance of sexuality owned and controlled by them was a radical act of resistance not only against White supremacy, which at the time did not consider rape an offense against Black women but also against patriarchy's prescription for how a respectable woman ought to conduct herself.[12] Black women employing (and subverting) indecency as rebellion on two fronts, if you will. Nearly one hundred years later, we see a repetition of such sexual defiance and subversion in the works of artists like Lil' Kim and Nicki Minaj, and groups like Salt-N-Pepa and TLC, further reiterating the staying power of Black Feminism and its ability to adjust to the needs of the times.

It was not just in the music—Black feminist themes also began to appear in Black women's literature and poetry, emerging during the Renaissance and continuing through today. Audre Lorde, critical Black feminist theorist and artist, first-generation Caribbean American, and member of the revolutionary Combahee River Collective, spoke to the essentiality of poetry for Black women:

> For women, then, poetry is not a luxury. It is a vital necessity of our existence. It forms the quality of light within which we predicate our hopes and dreams toward survival and change, first made into language, then into idea, then into more tangible action. Poetry is the way we help give name to the nameless so it can be thought. The farthest horizons of our hopes and fears are cobbled by our poems, carved from the rock experiences of our daily lives.[13]

Poetry is a kind of catch-and-release coping strategy, wherein the hell of racism and sexism is caught and then released into art, a skill honed by "free" Black women across postslavery generations. In the art of Lorde ("A Woman Speaks"), Sonia Sanchez ("Present"), and others, we have plenty of examples of Black women presenting Black womanhood as they have observed and experienced it, a standard practice of Black feminist women. In carrying on this tradition, these Black feminist artists spurred the movement forward while expanding its reach—art functioning as a conduit for liberatory messages is central to freedom work.

So it stands to reason that in the twenty-first century, Black feminist women would find yet another method for increasing awareness of the plight of Black women and sharing their experiences and gripes with the sexism and racism of the time. Enter the immediacy, access, and connectivity of social media platforms like Facebook, Twitter, and Instagram. The imperative to create and hold space for the often erased, generally ignored Black woman has reached its pinnacle and Black women's voices have been refreshingly explosive in the self-affirming, self-preserving digital communities we have formed. If our work until now has been a wade in the water, social media is God's troubling as our consciousness rages through the broken levies of systemic racism and toxic masculinity. Employing hashtags as meeting rooms and Twitter threads as public gathering spaces, Black women are pushing this long-standing fight to the forefront of the world's collective consciousness with little obstruction or censorship. Freedom of speech takes on a new meaning when those most denied access to the fundamental right are now proprietors of the most free discourse of our time. And when that discourse morphs into movements, and not only challenges the way people think but also how they behave, we can no longer deny the power of the Black feminist voice in reconstructing liberation narratives for both women and Black people.[14]

To the question of why Black women of today do not simply align themselves with modern White women, who outwardly appear to be making significant progress in the women's liberation movement, is of mild importance, but let's address it anyway. Mainstream White Feminism, as it is regularly referred to, continues to represent a hierarchy of womanhood that relies on the lingering putrid bastions of White supremacy and centers the oppression of the privileged. White women are oppressed, yes, and we know that their fight to dismantle male hegemony has been a protracted one. But in all of their attempts to "smash the patriarchy," there remains a white film of racist residue on the windows of their glass houses. Yes, a strong feminist movement is the antidote to patriarchy and a stronger feminist movement exists when *all* women collude, on equal footing, to present an impenetrable case against the validity of male supremacy.[15] Whose evidence is called upon when toxic masculinity is on trial and whose experiences are levied as fodder for strong arguments without appropriate credit being given to their particular circumstances? Black women. And when mainstream feminism tastes like unseasoned chicken at a patriotic Fourth of July barbecue, why would any Black woman feel compelled to bite into it?

I don't feel the need to elaborate on Black women not fully aligning ourselves with any modern iteration of the Black liberation movement, because we *are* it; we are the modern arbiters and architects of this fight. Before anyone gets upset, I am not saying that no one else is working this liberation space—truly there are some admirable people doing important

work to move us closer to Dr. King's promised land, and I stand in solidarity with them and support their work insofar as it centers more people
than it excludes. And while there are, and always have been, those who
purport to be about the business of Black liberation but see the "work" as a
means to an individually enterprising end, I don't really want to spend too
much time focusing on their nonsense outside of clowning it completely.
My focus is on Black women and our contributions to forward progress,
and I will repeatedly assert that our contribution to this painstaking work
is essential to *all* liberation work. Black Feminism/womanism (used inter-
changeably throughout) has become an affirming space for Black women
who reject the racism of mainstream White Feminism and the notorious
(hetero)sexism of the Black Power movement.

The use of hashtags on Twitter helps users find specific topics and associated social media posts. Like "#BlackTwitter," using the hashtag before the term "Black Feminism" is done more for the sake of discussion
than any consistent or practical use. In her 2014 dissertation, Dr. Meredith Clark, the first woman to write definitively about Black Twitter as
an online community, challenged many of the assumptions made about
how people identify and connect online when she "established a theoretical framework for exploring the multilevel community and network
building process commonly referred to as 'Black Twitter.'"[16] Her research
introduced Black Twitter to academia, in one significant way validating
the existence of a Black community and subculture on the social media
platform. Her dissertation outlined how Black users developed "an iden-
tifiable, influential meta-network of communicators with the ability to
impact news media coverage on Black American life." Few people actually use #BlackTwitter as a topic or trend; we simply acknowledge that
the community exists. And as Black Twitter functions as a broader, more
generalized cultural community space, Black Feminist Twitter exists as a
subculture of this notion of digital community. Dr. Clark elaborates on
how hashtags connect users:

> Twitter has the ability to connect people who may or may not have an
> online relationship through the asynchronous conversations formed via
> tweets. Anyone with Internet access can at least watch and track these

conversations, either by searching through Twitter feeds (a running post of tweets), or by searching for a specific hashtagged phrase. A hashtag, which may be connected to a single word or phrase, groups tweets, allowing users to use a keyword-search style approach to finding tweets about a specific topic.[17]

This explanation provides context for my focus on the use of hashtags by Black women.

For me, hashtags are a call to "Attention!"—like a whistle—that alerts people it is time to gather and participate in a community conversation about something, no matter if the topic is seriously important, humorously shady, or simply the latest entertainment gossip. Hashtags are not *required* to initiate or sustain these kinds of conversations, however.

Similarly, using a hashtag first does not mean a person should receive credit for conceptualizing an idea, movement, or campaign, as hashtag use can be rather arbitrary and haphazard. This is crucial to note, as there have been arguments over the origins of important ideas and the hashtags that later emerge. Yes, hashtags are powerful tools of engagement and function to attribute campaigns and movements to particular creators who deserve credit for their innovations, but they do not always signal original thought. Origin stories matter, and in a time when the conceptualization of noteworthy hashtags can make someone famous and written into the annals of history, we cannot allow for hashtags to erase the deep and creative impact of those who did not think to attach their work to a short, memorable phrase behind a # sign. For the most part, hashtags have been important mechanisms in modern movement-building, and Black women, Black feminist women especially, have exemplified best practices when it comes to hashtag utilization.

# CHAPTER 2

# #BlackFeminism 102

*I know that feeling that I feel when I see a black woman wake up, love herself, and go chase her dreams. That feeling for me is enough. It doesn't matter who's doing it, if they're well-known or not known at all. That's enough for me.*

—JUNGLEPUSSY, Brooklyn MC[1]

**MY FOCUS IS ON BLACK WOMEN** and the work of Black feminist women, but without the support of those who believe us, believe *in* us, want to right the wrongs against us, and who understand that there is no liberation of Black people without Black women, we would never be able to do what we do and be successful at it. Anyone who openly affirms Black Feminism as a powerfully transformative ideology and one that establishes a foundational blueprint for collective liberation is the real MVP. No one is perfect, and accepting that upfront upholds the humanity of the people doing this work. We learn, we grow, and we continue to challenge ourselves and each other to do and be better while continuing to educate those observing and looking up to us.

## MY PROBLEMATIC FAVS

Now, it seems like we think we have to be so competitive with each other and I feel like that's part of the main problem where they use that against us to divide us instead of bringing us together.

—RAPSODY, hip-hop MC[2]

"Problematic," as it describes someone these days, is supposed to mean that a person does or says things that are eyebrow-raising at best and wholly detrimental to humanity's forward progress at worst. Human beings fuck up, and no amount of education, sensitivity training, or exposure to new ideas or anecdotal experiences will overhaul our thought processes, our conversations, and our jokes. Existing with high visibility in public spaces means enduring immense scrutiny, and with social media exponentially increasing one's visibility as one's follower and subscriber counts rise, it can be hard to avoid being dragged for filth when you fuck up. (I have been on the receiving end of a dragging. It ain't fun.) Publicly owning up to a mistake and making an effort to do and be better is the best salve. *Publicly.* And therein lies the rub.

How many of us truly change how we think or shift our beliefs every single time we are exposed to new ideas? How often does being publicly called out simply silence us or push us into the shadows with our problematic thoughts? I know good and damned well that many of us quietly subscribe to some potentially harmful ideas and think dumb-ass thoughts, yet we only share them when we feel it's safe to do so. That's within the confines of private chat rooms, text messages with close friends and family, or in online spaces, behind fake avis and our own faux bravado. *Then* we get more open with our problematic ideas, jokes, and candor. I have learned *so* much by engaging with all kinds of people on social media who do this. I have learned about my own privileges, how to stop using certain words that are harmful and offensive, and how to accept that simply because I do not intend to do harm, I am incapable of doing harm. I need to be mindful of what I say and do—not only in public but in private, where I feel I can more comfortably be myself.

But can I keep it one hundred? Can we be really *real* here?

Some folks are and will continue to be "ain't shit" people. At least in some areas. Accepting this truth allows for more authentic engagement with each other as human beings, not as perfect role models, "fact portal mammies,"[3] or infallible icons. It allows us to get deeper into the uncomfortable truths about socialization, indoctrination, and the work it will take us to become better people overall. I ain't shit. You ain't shit. She ain't shit. Okay, great. Let's move forward with authentic growth and progress and rely less on dragging people as a deflection from our own skeleton-filled closets and more on openly (and respectfully) challenging each other's ideas as a method of engaging in impactful discourse.

With that said, when I think about the women who have made significant contributions to the most recent iteration of Black feminist thought and practice, they range from those with high-level education and years of experience doing gender work in academic and institutional spaces to those whose understanding and embrace of Black Feminism comes from their as-yet-to-be-substantiated-by-feminist-theory life experiences. All contributions are important, even if I do not agree with their ideas, if I think they are simply doing too much with the ways they read into things and the conclusions they draw or if I think they can benefit from more in-depth gender studies and readings on feminist theory. I am no one's bona fide expert on all things feminism, so it is not my place to assign value or rank contributions based on how feminist I think they are. Each contribution is important because it provides opportunities for broader discussions that may or may not begin with "Girl, what the fuck is this?"

Some of the best conversations on Twitter begin with someone presenting an idea so outlandish that it is impossible to resist responding to it. Oftentimes, the response leads to a threaded essay that not only challenges the thought presented but also provides evidential support, links to additional materials, and is a thoughtful, nuanced counterargument that benefits those who happen to be reading along. This is how knowledge is shared in these spaces, and those who act as participant observers often note how they are better for receiving such education. And since I *do* have quite a bit of knowledge through institutional education and lived experience, as well as substantial practical application and a body of work from which to draw in my arguments, I believe contributing my expertise to the discourse is significant and matters. I regard my peers similarly, so documenting and amplifying not only their words but their actions, advocacy, movements, campaigns, and offerings to the Black feminist canon is important work for me, and work I am more than happy to do.

I have learned that I do not have to agree with someone's approach or their style to honor the fact that they live in their truth and are helping push us all forward. I do not even have to talk to them to show them love. There are some really awful people out there masquerading as being pro-woman, pro-Black, or even feminist, and I can't abide by that nonsense. So when given the opportunity, I will honor and celebrate the various ways in which we *all* have the same goal of liberating Black women around the globe and creating a world in which being women and being Black (and every other thing we are) is no longer seen as a hindrance or obstacle but a pathway to a free existence as human beings. Each of these women has poured some aspect of herself into our collective movement, and that's love.

## STRAIGHT OUTTA HASHTAG FEMINISM

Some of the more prominent hashtags and campaigns that have changed the course of history have come from Black women who identify as feminist or womanist. One does not need a hashtag to build a movement or make change, but a few have helped move the needle forward.

#SolidarityIsForWhiteWomen reminded us that when it comes to working for *all* women, White women who claim to be feminist can often be found omitting women of color in their feminist advocacy. Specifically, when Black women face gender-based violence, being able to rely on White women for support is not something we expect or even seek to do. Too often, White women take up for the men, usually White, who enact violence against women of color, because racial solidarity continues to benefit them more than gender solidarity and has for well over a century of feminist work. In 2013, Mikki Kendall, the creator of the tag, explained:

> When I launched the hashtag #SolidarityIsForWhiteWomen, I thought it would largely be a discussion between people impacted by the latest bout of problematic behavior from mainstream white feminists. It was intended to be Twitter shorthand for how often feminists of color are told that the racism they experience "isn't a feminist issue." The first few tweets reflect the deeply personal impact of such a long-running structural issue.[4]

When White women remain silent when a high-profile White man is called to task for his violent treatment of Black women or a White

"feminist" musician plans a songwriting retreat at a former slave plantation, Black women experience a level of alienation that no woman fighting for women's rights should have to endure.[5] The act of calling out the
truth—that White feminist women can be really ignorant when it comes
to the experiences of women of color and how our racial identities are
integral to our womanhood—triggered such controversy that Kendall and
others, including Sydette Harry, who was a target of the violence about
which Kendall was initially speaking, began receiving vitriol on- and
offline. What started as a few tweets turned into an ongoing conversation
that lasted for days, then weeks, then months, and now years. The impact of #SolidarityIsForWhiteWomen has been enormous and Kendall has
been regarded as a thought leader on the topic. She already was, whether
or not people knew her name or recognized her prior work with *Hood
Feminism*, a blog that centered the experiences and ideas of women who
not only grew up in the "hood" but embraced more raw, no-nonsense approaches to women's equality and Black women's feminist evolution. But
this hashtag brought her voice, and those of other women of color who
have felt excluded from feminist solidarity, to the fore. I would go so far
as to argue that her use of this hashtag in 2013 spurred the use of hashtags
as more than simply tools of categorization but also as vehicles for creating
campaigns, movements, and accessible public discourse.

Violence against women has been thrust to the forefront of our minds,
our news, and our legislation more than it ever has been prior to the
turn of the century. While feminists have always championed victims of
gender-based violence, to endure physical, sexual, financial, and emotional
violence is something too many women have come to expect simply by
existing as women. According to the World Health Organization, at least
30 percent of all women have experienced some form of sexual or physical
violence in their lifetimes and 38 percent of all murders of women are
committed by a male intimate partner.[6] Despite advances made in gender
equity, with women earning more college degrees, achieving higher-level
career positions, and being financial heads of more households than ever
before, women and girls continue to be vulnerable to the violent intentions
of men, worldwide. One reason we know way more now than we ever did
about the statistics and anecdotes related to violence against women is how

the news and information travels via social media. I'm not sure that we are witnessing a rise in violence against women; data suggests violence against women has declined significantly in the last couple of decades.[7] What is actually happening is that we are becoming more exposed to acts of violence because the way news is reported has changed and more women have been encouraged to share their stories openly and publicly. As more women are talking about the violence they have endured, it can seem as if it is happening more; social media participation has that effect on how we process news that is shared 24/7, on nearly every platform we access.

It takes a great deal of courage to admit to yourself or even your friends and family that you have been a victim of violence. To admit it to complete strangers in public arenas, where anyone with any kind of intention has access, is an even braver act. Social media has facilitated this level of sharing for many women who have experienced gender-based harassment, assault, and other forms of violence. There have been a number of hashtags created to not only initiate discussion about these experiences but also to offer community space for support and healing, with many participants sharing their stories for the first time ever. While social media exposes you to anyone and everyone, it also gives a user a cloak of anonymity through taking a chosen name, having few followers, and being able to share and go. For some, just simply being able to say what happened "out loud" helps them begin their journey of healing. For others, finding solidarity with others who have experienced something similar serves to alleviate a lot of their stress and internalization of blame. And as we have seen with the resurgence of Tarana Burke's #MeToo movement, collective, supported, and corroborated public testimony can lead to perpetrators being held accountable for the harm they have caused others.

In the summer of 2014, I witnessed a familiar scene: A woman was walking and a man was trying too hard to get her attention, to the point where he began harassing her. I was with my son and she was pushing a stroller. I observed the interaction for a few minutes, but as it continued on, I could tell she was uncomfortable and he was becoming a pain in the ass. I felt compelled to see if she was OK. So I asked, "You OK, sis?" Though my question was directed at her, he took my interference as an affront. The woman meanwhile thanked me and whisked her baby away from the scene, seemingly grateful for the intervention. I continued to interact with the man, who felt disrespected and condemned me for interrupting him. I really didn't give a fuck, in part because I was old enough to be his mother but mainly because I have dealt with this kind of street harassment since I was eleven years old, though usually it was way more vulgar than what I witnessed.

Later that afternoon, I logged onto Twitter and shared the story of what happened. When I was done, I asked everyone reading if they could join me in making that kind of intervention a "thing"—could everyone who witnessed street harassment against women at least ask the victim if she was OK? There was a lot of support for the idea, and the hashtag #YouOKSis came about within a few minutes.

First:

---

RT **@rnboskye:** @FeministaJones I'm with you. Summer, the beginning of #YouOKSis?

💬          🔁          ♡

---

Then:

---

RT **@BlackGirlDanger:** @FeministaJones Can this be a thing? Can we, like, start a national #YouOKSis? Campaign?[8]

💬          🔁          ♡

---

Again, origin stories matter, so I would be remiss if I did not make clear how the hashtag #YouOKSis evolved. The idea of an online movement was mine, based on an experience I had and my desire to make a societal change. It was in amplifying my message that a blogger and active Twitter user, Mia Mackenzie (formerly @BlackGirlDanger), first used the tag, though she has shied away from taking any credit for it, but I cannot deny her contribution.[9]

Immediately, people began responding to the thread, agreeing to join in and do their part to intervene when they witnessed similar situations. The conversation caught the attention of journalist Terrell Starr, who

offered to write an article and do a video about the concept. He interviewed several Black women in New York City for the report and, in
partnership with *NewsOne* media, we hosted a town hall–style chat about
Black and Latina women's experiences with street harassment that July. I
centered Black and Latina women because, until that point, the majority
of anti–street harassment activism had been led by White women and they
had become the face of it. I felt it was important to challenge that narrative, especially knowing that violent street harassment is more likely to be
experienced by women of color than by White women. Queen Latifah
brought attention to the nuanced experience of Black women when it
comes to street harassment in her song "U.N.I.T.Y.," asking rejected and
ignored men on the street, "Who you callin' a bitch?" Before that, Janet
Jackson addressed street harassment in her song "Nasty." Both women
have said they wrote the songs after experiencing street harassment, and
the way they shared about it was culturally relevant and specific. Beyond
that, there has been little in the mainstream centering the experiences of
women of color.

The hashtag and campaign garnered a lot of attention not just on Twitter and not just in the United States. Women as far as South Africa embraced the movement, and the more media outlets reported on it, the
more word spread and the movement grew.[10] Over time, it grew to include
women sharing stories of other forms of gender-based abuse and violence,
but for the most part it has continued to center women of color and remains relevant today. Street harassment is on the spectrum of the kinds of
violence women experience, as is sexual harassment at work, so #MeToo
and #YouOKSis function in tandem to combat the daily bullshit women
deal with outside of their homes. What goes on inside the home is another
issue entirely, and speaking up about intimate-partner/spousal violence
is often met with such denial, erasure, and vitriol that it is any wonder
women bother to complain at all. An estimated 57 percent of all mass
shootings are related to domestic violence, with many of the instances involving a man attempting to (and succeeding at) killing his partner and/or
their children and other members of their family or close friends who happen to be in the vicinity.[11] And with more than twenty thousand calls per
day to domestic violence hotlines from the estimated ten million people

who experience some form of intimate-partner violence, the matter continues to plague our society.[12]

An estimated three women die each day as a result of domestic violence, and because Black women die as a result of this violence at a rate almost three times that of White women, we can make an educated assumption that at least one of those women is Black.[13] In 2014, Beverly Gooden, a Black feminist woman, launched the hashtag #WhyIStayed to address the issue. We often hear people say, in reaction to finding out women remain with abusive partners, "Why did she stay?" It is a victim-blaming tactic that places the burden of responsibility for violence on the women. Gooden challenged the notion by explaining why she stayed in an abusive relationship, and other people joined in, sharing their own stories and experiences.[14] The hashtag opened up the conversation about why it is not simple or easy to leave a violent relationship and became one of the top feminist hashtags of the year. As is often the case, Black women's experiences with intimate-partner violence have not been prominent in news reporting. Cheryl "Salt" James, one half of the iconic hip-hop duo Salt-N-Pepa, emphasized the importance of speaking out about abuse. "I think the key to changing the kind of abuse and inequality women have had to live with is that we have to talk about it with one another, and be there for one another and support one another."[15] The rapper Eve also spoke about domestic violence when she chronicled the story of losing her close friend, who stayed with an abusive man, to domestic violence in her 1999 hit "Love Is Blind." The song offered a poignant, necessary perspective, as women who live in poverty and the hood experience intimate-partner violence at seven times the rate of those who do not. She raps about her best friend being under the power of a man who repeatedly abused her and eventually killed her. Her storytelling connected with women who needed to receive a dose of reality and encouragement to seek help if they are being abused.

Since the launch of the campaign, Gooden has been able to speak at events and conferences, on panels, and host workshops all with the aim of reducing the shame too many survivors of domestic violence experience.[16] Inspired by her work and the work of other brave women, I began documenting instances of intimate-partner violence, primarily enacted against women of color, as they appeared in the news. I felt it important to acknowledge them and share their stories because of the gross underreporting and, over a couple of years, managed to document over eighty cases. After all, if Black women don't speak up for Black women, who will?

## LEADING THE FIGHT FOR ALL BLACK PEOPLE

#BlackLivesMatter was popularized and made into a global movement by Patrisse Cullors, Alicia Garza, and Opal Tometi, three Black women who were activists and advocates in their own rights prior to collaborating on this effort. I use the term "popularized" because, despite being credited by the Pew Research Center and other sources with being the hashtag's originators, they were not the first to use it.[17] That distinction goes to Dr. Marcus Anthony Hunter, who tweeted it on August 20, 2002:

---

**@manthonyhunter:** check out amazing articles by @jean23bean and aldon morris new ed of @contextsmag #blacklivesmatter.[18]

---

Again, origin stories matter. Crediting Cullors, Garza, and Tometi with the first use of the #BlackLivesMatter hashtag is incorrect. But more than that, it is incomplete. Instead, Cullors should be credited with using the hashtag in a way that launched a modern movement, and that because of how she, Garza, and Tometi shaped it as a rallying cry, we now have a new and concise way of affirming Black humanity in the twenty-first century. Their call to arms was indisputably influential: in the first three years since they began using the hashtag, it was tweeted nearly twelve million times and, according to Pew, is the third-most-used hashtag in Twitter history.[19]

Since 2013, "Black Lives Matter" (or BLM for short) has transformed into a decentralized movement of activist groups around the world who engage in modern challenges to the racist status quo, calling on the support of people of all races and genders, all classes, every religion, and of every socioeconomic status. Arguably the most cohesive modern Black liberation movement, Black Lives Matter sparked a fire in dormant hearts, forcing people everywhere to recognize systemic violence against Black people across the diaspora and motivating them to take some sort of action to combat it. Critics assert that Black Lives Matter is an anti-White terrorist group; the counterargument, "All Lives Matter," is little more than a racist dog whistle that attempts to both delegitimize centuries of claims of global anti-Black oppression and position those who exhibit tremendous pride in their Blackness as enemies of the state. Well, we *are* enemies of any racist, sexist, classist, xenophobic state that sanctions brutality and murder against marginalized people who deserve to live as free people. It is simply considered a radical notion to identify Black lives as ones that hold value beyond serving as an exploitable labor force.

In the months after the launch of BLM as an organized movement, other groups emerged as supporters of the idea that Black lives matter, though not necessarily an output or direct affiliate of Black Lives Matter the organization. The Movement for Black Lives (#M4BL), for example, began with a July 2015 gathering in Cleveland of over fifty activist groups (including members of Black Lives Matter chapters), all invested in Black liberation and in ending racist tyranny against Black people around the world. In the year following, the M4BL, with nearly 150,000 individual and organizational endorsements, developed a policy platform with demands that included an end to the war on Black people, reparations, and economic justice.[20] We The Protesters, helmed by DeRay Mckesson, Brittany Packnett, and Samuel Sinyangwe, was formed in response to and in support of the protests in Ferguson, Missouri, immediately after the killing of an unarmed Black teenager, Michael Brown, by Ferguson police on August 9, 2014.[21] In the days after his death, several protests and demonstrations took place not only in the United States, but around the world. Women like Johnetta Elzie, Brittany Packnett, and Cherrell Brown organized in Ferguson, galvanizing those who were frustrated but had little organizational experience or expertise.[22] These women, along with supporters of all genders and races, brought Ferguson to social media, the nightly news, and newspapers around the world, relying primarily on social media to document and share what was happening on the ground.

Activist momentum had been building since a twenty-two-year-old unarmed African American, Oscar Grant, was killed by an Oakland police officer in 2009. This was the first time I recall Twitter being used as a platform to raise massive awareness about police brutality in the United States, and I believe Grant's was the first name used in a hashtag to bring attention to Black men and women killed by the police.[23] The movement swelled, from protests against the police policy of stop-and-frisk in New York City in the summer of 2012, to response to the 2013 murder of Trayvon Martin by White supremacist George Zimmerman in Florida, which served as the catalyst for the launch of BLM. By the time Brown was killed, Black folks had had enough.

As we grew more disgusted with the blatant disregard for Black humanity, and the stories of Black people being killed by police officers increased, the energy coalesced in many spaces and on many stages, driven in large part by Black women. By the time We The Protesters launched Campaign Zero, a "data-informed platform present[ing] comprehensive solutions to end police violence in America," several groups had presented similar platforms, and the work was pushed forward by determined and committed Black women (Brown, Elzie, Packnett, and others).[24] Remember when the Confederate flag was removed from the South Carolina statehouse in 2015? A Black feminist woman, Bree Newsome, completed that awesome feat and was recognized and widely celebrated for her rebellious defiance against the most pervasive symbol of America's history of White supremacy. What she did was so dope that she not only received well-deserved awards, she was also included in a rap song by the legendary hip-hop group A Tribe Called Quest, who make reference to her climb to the top of the statehouse in the song "Space Program." Iconic, truly.

In 2018, Cullors announced that she, Tometi, and Garza were no longer sharing responsibility for the leadership of Black Lives Matter. Garza and Tometi stepped down from leadership roles in the daily operations of the organization while Cullors continued on, serving as senior strategist and global spokesperson.[25] Fortunately, the news of their disbanding didn't make the kinds of waves that would disrupt the work being done to end state violence against Black people. In the four years of activism in and around BLM, so many people have been empowered to do *something* and make contributions to the movement as a whole, even if not under the "Black Lives Matter" banner.

In 2014, one such person was me. When Eric Garner was killed by New York police that summer, the anger was palpable, and demonstrations were popping up all around. Having been an organizer and activist/protester for more than fifteen years at that point, I began to assess the impact of these demonstrations and recognized that we, as a people, would need to be more organized in our efforts to call to an end to police brutality. This is not to say that fighting police brutality was new or that there was a complete lack of organization, but there was a growing interest, particularly among younger people and folks newer to activist spaces, in becoming more actively involved in organized efforts to rebel. So when Brown was killed in August, I saw people wanting to take to the streets. On Twitter and Facebook, people were beginning to organize meet-ups, rallies, and other demonstrations in protest of his killing. At the time, I lived in the Bronx and saw two women discussing planning a demonstration on a Sunday evening in lower Manhattan. It bothered me because most of the people directly affected by police violence in New York City lived nowhere near the proposed meeting place, and to hold it on a Sunday evening, for people who would likely have to travel by train from far distances on a day when the transit system was operating on a reduced schedule, did not make logistical sense. Again, I was thinking like an organizer, fresh off the momentum of my anti–street harassment campaign, #YouOKSis. I reached out to them, expressing my concern about their plans, and offered to organize a larger event, accessible to more people and in more places for the greatest impact. I immediately solicited Twitter's interest in such a movement and on the afternoon of August 10, 2014, #NMOS14, or the National Moment of Silence 2014, was launched. At the time, I believe I had about 28,000 followers or so, which was not too shabby at the time, so I knew that I would be able to reach a lot of people with the idea. Using Twitter, Facebook, and Instagram, and working with close to a hundred people (including organizers from Freedom Side, a grassroots organization that was working on strategic planning and developing templates for direct actions), I was able to coordinate over 119 vigils that took place five days after Brown was killed, in forty-two states and five countries.[26] This is the power of hashtag feminism.

Several of the people who attended or organized those vigils were inspired and motivated to get further involved in the overall movement, including DeRay Mckesson (We The Protesters, Campaign Zero) and Leslie McFadden (Ferguson Response Network, Safety Pin Box). Approximately 80 percent of the organizers had never worked on any type of protest action or organized any such gathering, and *that* was, in my opinion, the greatest result of #NMOS14. In the tradition of Ella Baker, a civil rights movement activist known for her ability to empower everyday people into direct action, I was able to decentralize control of civil rights actions and shift from the single-charismatic-leader model to an approach in which everyday people took ownership of activism and found their voices and skills as they worked to fight oppression. By our best guess, over a hundred thousand people participated in vigils that day, with some cities like Chicago and New York seeing as many as three thousand to five thousand participants each, and even more felt the impact of the gathering. Those of us who did the work will never forget how we brought people around the country and world together for one day of solidarity (still, to date, the largest demonstration against police brutality in the US in the twenty-first century).

The movement to end police brutality has, unfortunately, fallen into the same sexist patterns of previous civil rights and Black Power movements. Ask most people familiar with Black Lives Matter to name five Black men killed by police in the last five years and I would bet money that the majority of them can quickly rattle off names. Ask those same people to name five Black women and they won't make it much further than "Sandra Bland."[27] Most people cannot easily name at least five Black women killed by police because Black women simply do not garner the same attention and support when they experience police violence. And if it is a trans woman? Forget it. You may *never* learn of her death or assault. Andrea Ritchie, an attorney specializing in police misconduct, explores the history of state-sanctioned violence against Black women in her 2017 book *Invisible No More*.[28] She writes that Black women have been subjected to uniquely cruel acts of violence, including institutionalized rape, that have been upheld by law, rendering void the idea that we can seek help from the police. Ritchie discusses sexual violence against women of color at the hands of the police and holds critical space for trans women who have been subjected to police brutality, a radical move, even for our time.[29] The erasure of Black women from the overall narrative about police brutality echoes the sexism of the 1960s and 1970s, a time when Black women were often relegated to serving as anonymous workers, being controlled as concubines (fuck Eldridge Cleaver and everything that nigga ever did), removed from major protest events, and being forced to walk separately from and behind men at major marches and demonstrations.[30] You would think, after all of these years and after so many male leaders being assassinated and locked up, that Black women would be respected as leaders and included in every aspect of liberation work.

Nope. Still not happening. Malcolm X famously said that the Black woman is the most disrespected woman in America. He wasn't lying . . . at all. And we see that even now. Black women continue to be excluded from prevailing narratives about state-sanctioned violence, so what do we do? Create campaigns to honor their lives, demand action be taken when they face oppression, and call attention to their deaths. Kimberlé Crenshaw, the lawyer, professor, and all-around dope-ass sista who acts as executive director of the African American Policy Forum and gave us the language of "intersectionality," thus thrusting us forward in our feminist praxis, created the #SayHerName campaign to honor the most forgotten victims: women. Launched in the spring of 2015, #SayHerName calls on us to amplify the names of Black women and girls who have been victims of police violence. It is a rallying cry that demands equal attention be paid to women and girls, who not only experience fatal police violence just as Black men do, we are also regularly subjected to sexual harassment and violence from police.

Unfortunately, patriarchy gets in the way of Black women's deaths being amplified, because a Black woman being killed by police is a reminder that the Black man cannot protect the Black woman from harm. Since enslavement, at least, Black men have been forced to watch as Black women have been repeatedly brutalized by White people, unable to demonstrate their manhood in the most primal way: protecting women. Historically, when a Black man attempted to intervene and help/defend a Black woman from oppressive violence, he made himself vulnerable to persecution leading up to death.[31] Over generations, the defeated embrace of this reality may be the cause of Black men being hesitant to put themselves out there when Black women face racist oppression; they feel both helpless to do anything and know that their involvement puts them at personal risk. With that, public acknowledgment of Black women's persecution, primarily by White men with the support of the state, is public acknowledgment of their own demasculinization.[32] I do not think this is a simple matter to be dismissed, and my hope is that the discourse and action around #SayHerName will bring more of these causes to the forefront of conversation and push us to collectively address the lack of support and the silencing of Black women's pain and suffering at the hands of police.

#BringBackOurGirls, a movement created in response to terrorist group Boko Haram's kidnapping of hundreds of girls in Chibok, Nigeria, was created by feminist Nigerian activist Obiageli Ezekwesili. While she was not the first person to use the hashtag, its use was inspired by her call to action to rescue and bring the girls back. Her plea would eventually be echoed by millions across the globe, including former First Lady of the United States Michelle Obama. The hashtag awakened a consciousness about the violence inflicted on women and girls in the region and dominated the news and media for weeks.[33] In 2015, I was able to meet Ezekwesili in London and she was incredibly inspiring in her commitment to the work (and even told me she admires my work! I died. I live!). Since the 2014 kidnapping, several of the girls and women escaped or were released, though the whereabouts of more than one hundred remain in question, and most are feared dead.[34] Still, the efforts continue, and Ezekwesili has maintained that she will not give up until as many of the girls as possible are returned home safely.

There are so many more examples of how Black feminists have been doing the damned thing when it comes to shaking the table, creating sustainable discourse, and launching movements that reverberate around the world. The examples included here cover three key areas where Black women's representation has not only been much-needed, but completely game-changing: feminist framework, Black liberation, and sociocultural identity. Blackness and womanhood no longer function as liabilities to individual progress, but rather assets that make for groundbreaking changes and paradigm shifts. We have seen it in Brazil, where Black women have been organizing in some of the most progressive and radical ways at 2016's Black Feminisms Forum and with movements like #MeuPrimeiroAssedio ("My first harassment"), and across Africa, with #AfriFem, #Caster (for Caster Semenya, a South African woman subjected to horrific gender-based oppression), Kenyan activist Ory Okolloh's #147notjusta number, #BeingFemaleInNigeria, and #RhodesMustFall. We have seen it with our disabled sistas who call out racism in disability activism. Keah Brown gave us the beauty of #DisabledAndCute, and there is the work of Vilissa Thompson, social worker and creator of "Ramp Your Voice," a self-advocacy and empowerment movement for people with disabilities, and the #DisabilitySoWhite hashtag, with which she and others amplify the unique experiences of disabled people of color.

When Tara L. Conley created the website Hashtag Feminism, it was because she noticed that a number of hashtags created by feminists or related to feminism were dominating conversations on Twitter:

> Twitter has been a contentious and transformative space for feminist discourse. There are still folks out there whose day job it is to demonize feminists/feminism—most of whom hide behind Twitter eggs. But I also know that if it weren't for hashtags like #YouOKSis, #Solidarity IsForWhiteWomen, #WhyIStayed, #RapeCultureIsWhen, #Free Marissa, all of the #IStandWith tags, and tags that called attention to the deaths of black women like #RenishaMcBride and #SandraBland, and all those under the #SayHerName tag—we would likely be having very different public conversations, or worse, no conversations.[35]

Among the two dozen hashtags referenced in a 2016 article as influential in shaping the discussion around feminism, ten were created by Black women: #GirlsLikeUs, #SolidarityIsForWhiteWomen, #Black GirlsAreMagic, #PrettyPeriod, #WhyIStayed, #BringBackOurGirls, #Rape CultureIsWhen, #YouOKSis, #ToTheGirls, and #EffYourBeautyStandards.[36] From policy making to picture taking, Black women continue to change the way we approach, engage, and experience so many of the things we once took for granted in our daily lives.[37] From the tweets to the world's streets, Black women continually do the hard work of challenging the status quo, shaping culture, advocating for social, economic, and political advancement and equality for women, and building community.

CHAPTER 3

# Thread!

**I HAVE BEEN USING VARIOUS** forms of social media for about two decades. It started with America Online in 1997 with my first username, "MBenee18." I was eighteen years old and my mother told me all about this service that allowed you to use your phone to dial into the World Wide Web. I would wait patiently as my computer connected to the internet by way of our home landline and feel the excitement of being able to talk to people from all over the world. While much of my early online use was playing games like spades and poker, I slowly began to venture into the chat rooms, where you could interact with complete strangers. At first, I would go to the general chat rooms, grouped by age or location, because I figured I'd have the most in common with older teens from New York City. After a year or so of answering the "A/S/L?" question a million times (that's age/sex/location for you newbies), I looked for more specific groups with unique interests.

I was drawn to chat rooms that focused on BBW—Big Beautiful Women—where I was introduced to an entire world of people who were either plus-sized themselves or romantically interested in women of larger sizes. The ages varied but trended older, and I was among the youngest in the groups. That did little to stop me from being outspoken and engaging. This was a space that was mostly affirming of women who society rejected and cast aside, so to see such adoration and praise for our aesthetic was invigorating. We grew close as a niche "family," and every day, we looked forward to hopping online and chatting with each other, sometimes for hours on end. We would discuss everything from sex to politics, and it was really interesting to learn more about how thirtysomething women from California and Texas felt about their bodies, their experiences with dating, and their thoughts on whether or not we'd ever have a Black or female president. We even connected offline, arranging parties and other meetup events in cities like New York City, Las Vegas, and Washington, DC. For the first time in my life, I felt seen and heard, and safe in the knowledge that I would not be ridiculed or completely ignored for being a plus-sized Black woman.

What really drew me into online chatting, though, was the overwhelmingly warm embrace of Black sisterhood. Having attended a predominantly White boarding school where I was one of only five Black female students in my graduating class, I longed for a broader, organic connection to Black women. I met two of my closest friends in high school, so it wasn't all bad, but I think living in isolation from positive Black female influence took a toll on me at a time when I was actively seeking relationships with other women. Life was difficult for me at that time—I'd taken time off from school before committing to another years-long educational journey, and I wasn't exactly sure who or what I wanted to be and where I was heading next. I was reconciling traumas I'd experienced throughout my short life, mostly related to sexual abuse and assault, and it was around this time that I began experiencing my first major bouts of depression and suicidal ideation. My relationship with my mother was strained and my father was there, but not in the ways I needed or wanted, and I did not have the courage to ask for more from him. I was craving nurturing, support, mentoring, and guidance that could only come from Black women who, perhaps, had more worldly experiences. I grew up fearing older Black women because they represented judgment, harsh words, beatings, and ridicule, often in the name of Jesus. While it would be a while before I learned more about why some of the women in my family behaved in these ways, I knew that my connection to the Black matriarch archetype was rooted more in trauma than in loving affirmation. I found these seemingly strong and empowered women congregating online and, after a few months of chatting, I felt accepted into their extended family.

This was also around the time I began to come into my identity as a Black feminist woman. I'd been inspired by the "girl power" anthems of my youth and I'd been able to study a few amazing women in some of my high school English electives, but I had not fully delved into critical feminist theory, particularly the work of Black feminist scholars like Angela Davis, Patricia Hill Collins, Michelle Wallace, or the participants of the Combahee River Collective. In the year I took off between high school and college, I began reading and studying more of their works because I did not want to slow my intellectual progress, despite not having any solid college plans. From the beginning, the theme of sisterly reliance stood out to me, and Black women connecting through conversations, activism, church, and community-based work stood out as powerful to me. I was living that experience in the chat rooms, which served as a communal gathering space for women, mostly Black, mostly ostracized for one aesthetic reason or another, to build and hold space for each other. This was my first exposure to digital Black sisterhood and, as clichéd as it sounds, it changed me forever. Every chat room I actively participated in was dominated by the voices of Black women, and I felt that I had finally found a place to call "home."

Some people may not remember the earlier chat rooms on AOL or sites like BlackPlanet.[1] Here's how they worked: when you logged on, your name would pop up showing that you'd entered the room. If you were popular, you were met with several "Welcome!" greetings from the regulars, and if you weren't popular, you'd still have some folks, the resident greeters, welcoming you into the space. You would spend a few minutes catching up on whatever the topic of the moment was, and if you felt inclined, you would add your own commentary. You could change the font size, type, and color of your posts, and set yourself apart that way. I learned an early lesson about branding back then: I, "MBenee18" on AOL and later "missbenee" on BlackPlanet, was bold, italicized orange and everyone knew it. You were able to send private messages to people in the chat who would pop up on your screen and theirs, but no one else could see. You could reply directly to people or mention them in your chat lines to let them know you were addressing what they said. You could post pictures to convey a thought or reaction. You could also block people from being able to contact you, which alleviated a lot of the negativity that was inevitable in such a gathering space. The chat lines would scroll up at a speed determined by your internet connection, so you could follow along with the conversations, reading them line by line.

It was very much a call-and-response dynamic, and I began to think that maybe this was why Black women so successfully connected with each other in these spaces. I argue that call-and-response, as rooted in traditional African cultural communication, is inherent to Black women's speech patterns across the diaspora. It makes sense to me, then, that platforms designed to encourage a call-and-response style of communication would draw in Black women, especially, and would be ripe for evolution through our contributions. As Twitter is designed to foster conversation by using the "@" sign, long recognized as the word "at" in internet language, the premise is structured around the idea of speaking "at" someone, as opposed to speaking with someone. One person types something and to respond, users have to direct their typed words "at" them in their responses. If others bear witness to the exchange, they, too, can respond "at" the original call or to the subsequent responses. Call-and-response generally involves a person or group of people communicating in one way and a person or group of people responding directly to—or "at"—that initial communication in a way that often acknowledges the "call." In the majority of exchanges, the response affirms the call by offering a word of agreement or a positive sound that provides background emphasis, but sometimes, the response challenges or questions the call. The response may inspire or infuriate the caller, whose flow is largely contingent upon the kind of response it generates. It is an exchange, so there is, arguably, an occasional noticeable shift between who acts as the caller and who acts as the respondent. Ultimately, this is a collaborative experience in which exchanges are necessary and participants are connected through an innate understanding of this ebb and flow.

For Black people, the best example of this exchange can be found in charismatic houses of worship, mostly those of Christian denominations. A preacher stands in a pulpit or at the front of the church and delivers a sermon punctuated by the responses of the congregation. Similar to the Black pastor's sermonized "word," often presented with a sing-song cadence, a tweet functions as an antiphon (a sung biblical verse) shouted from a tweeter's pulpit or timeline/feed. As such, quote tweeting and retweeting are, as a cultural practice, antiphony or the singing/chanting of hymnal verses simultaneously by at least two different voices, making Twitter a forum rooted in the African call-and-response tradition. It makes sense, then, that Black women are the prominent figures in the medium, as we are the primary conduits of antiphony; we fill the pews and are the ones heard responding to and supporting the collaboration between preacher and congregants during Sunday sermons through call-and-response. Our retweets are our congregational "amens," whereas quote tweets (retweets with added commentary) or direct responses are our community's immediate response to the word through their own immediate interpretations. As one of us pieces together and presents our "sermons," others participate by echoing our words (retweeting), amplifying the message by cosigning it (quote tweeting), and engaging in the development of the message, even influencing its direction as we immediately and directly influence the originator's train of thought (direct response).

Dr. Ashon T. Crawley, author of *Blackpentecostal Breath: The Aesthetics of Possibility*, helped me flesh out the idea of "tweeting as antiphony" when I presented my initial thoughts to him. "I think antiphony names a cultural tradition in general," he shared, "and the way Black folks have experienced the sacred post-1661, it makes sense to me that the cultural and the religious are interrelated, that even if antiphony was about religion, because of the way the sacred and secular interarticulate each other for Black folks, that distinction does not hold. Everything, in other words, is cultural."[2] With so many Black cultural traditions and sociopolitical developments being deeply rooted in the Church, we understand why and how our mannerisms and inclinations can be directly connected to the Church beyond the religiosity, calling upon the culturally African traditions of praise and celebration, moving into the realm of even a religious practice.

This also makes me think of the hip-hop cypher, which is a gathering of MCs, often positioned in a circle that allows everyone included to be seen and heard. In the cypher, MCs come together to share their freestyled or memorized rhymes. In some instances, there are competitions, often called battles, wherein MCs deliver several lines that challenge their opponents to retort with wittier lines. The exchange continues until one person bows out or one person is declared the winner by the crowd gathered around to witness the exchange. The lines are delivered in succession and riff off of the ones that have come before it. The most skilled MCs can float out lines off the top of their heads that connect via cadence and rhyme, one poetic line to the next, to a crowd eagerly awaiting what comes next. The cypher, then, serves as another example of call-and-response communication developed primarily by Black Americans and preserved by those who have adopted this style of performative communication for themselves.

So goes the idea of the "Twitter thread."

When Twitter began, each tweet was limited to 140 characters to accommodate mobile accessibility—if standard text messages sent via mobile devices were limited to 160 characters, Twitter's developers wanted to make sure a single tweet could be sent/received through mobile devices without exceeding one message.[3] Each user could create a name limited to 20 characters, and this format reinforced brevity as a powerful tool and forced Twitter users to communicate in concise ways. For the verbose (ahem, me), this was incredibly difficult, but I adjusted. At first, I did not mind it as much because I did not really have much to say or share, and I was still tied to Facebook's format, which asked you to update your friends on what you were doing. Many of my early Facebook posts read, "Michelle is doing laundry" or, "Michelle is feeling like throwing her whole life away and starting over." (Michelle is my given name.) When I created my Twitter account, my very first tweet read, "@Purplepeace79 . . . recovering," a comment on my then-recent separation from my now ex-husband and my attempt to create a new social media profile that he could not access and that I could use to express myself in what I assumed was simply a new journaling platform.[4] I updated my Twitter statuses as duplicates of my Facebook statuses, and without many followers, I did not expect much engagement.

Honestly, I did not really understand how Twitter worked at first and had to ask around. Once I figured it out, though, I realized how innovative it really was. As I began to engage with more people and share my work, I began to tweet more frequently, and I remember feeling incredibly limited by the allowed character count. So, I did what anyone else would do: I began tweeting multiple tweets in succession and would direct people to read my entire timeline for my complete thoughts, whole stories, and for context. Many of us were longtime bloggers who were now participating in what was being called "microblogging," and it was changing the way we wrote and communicated in digital spaces. Redirecting someone to read your entire timeline for context wasn't always a surefire way to get people to read your writing, and expanding your thoughts in a blog entry was becoming less and less useful because people were becoming used to these short snippets of thought and commentary. Many of my blogs were no longer receiving the same kind of traction, and I realized that if I wanted people to grasp the fullness of my thoughts, I had to put them on Twitter, where folks had the immediate access they'd become accustomed to. Sure, I could give a snippet and link to a blog post, but were people actually reading? Some were, but it was clear in the responses that people were barely skimming, if they even clicked the links. If I, and other bloggers and writers like me, had a message to share, we had to present it in a series of linked tweets that reached people immediately and directly. As such, many Twitter threads, when expanded, read like long-form blog posts. I also realized that this was helpful for me because my sex-positive blog was often blocked from my followers' places of employment due to the "adult" content on it. Threading became a simple solution to a growing issue of reader engagement, and it remains a staple of Twitter communication.

In 2017, Twitter "officially" made threading part of its platform, after testing the code for some time. At first, it tested letting users type out their entire essay—ahem, thread—and post it in full, after which it would appear in a series of tweets all at once.[5] That wasn't as popular, so it evolved into how it is now—users can click "add another tweet" and continue their threads that way.

Prior to threading as we know it now, in 2014 Twitter's support page gave instructions for how to create a thread by replying to your own tweets. Some articles, including one in *The Verge*, tell this same story, attributing the popularity of Twitter threads to venture capitalist Marc Andreessen, who was known for linking tweets on his timeline.[6] Many users and reporters call threads "tweet storms," and the term suggests that a user is flooding the timeline with a long stream of thoughts that needs to be read in full for a complete understanding of the main point. I never liked the term "tweet storm," because it makes it seem as though people are imposing their thoughts on others, as opposed to simply sharing their own thoughts on their own timelines in a way that makes the most sense to them. Several articles reference popular White male tweeters and their tweet storms, citing them as the reason linking tweets became popular. But this is not true and is yet another example of how Black women's innovation is erased from narratives.

To wit: at least as early as December 2013, Twitter user @TheTrudz linked her tweets together by replying to herself. She realized that by doing this, she could connect her tweets together and when people clicked the original tweet to read it, they would see her replies, and thus her "thread" of tweets. Could someone before @TheTrudz have done this also? Perhaps. Could @TheTrudz and Andreessen have started linking tweets near the same time? Possibly. But @TheTrudz is not mentioned in the same breath as Andreessen as an innovator. And remember, origin stories matter.

I recall seeing @TheTrudz's threads and being blown away by her ingenuity. Until then, those of us who used multiple tweets to get a complete idea or story out relied on services like Storify, a now-defunct platform that allowed social media users to create "stories" compiled of tweets, Facebook posts, articles online, and the like with a few clicks and drags. Once you finished collecting all of your posts and compiling them, you had one complete piece that read very much like a critical essay or blog, and it could be more easily shared on platforms other than Twitter. With @TheTrudz's brilliant threading technique, though, we no longer had to compile our tweets on another site, and people could access our thoughts with one click and a few scrolls.

Over the years, Black women have continued to tinker with Twitter as a platform, creating ways to communicate that are more in line with our own norms. In response, Twitter has adapted its platform to how *we* tweet, from creating the current mechanism for threading to incorporating GIFs in tweet options. Even after they allowed for double the number of characters per tweet, people were still threading their tweets because we had the same amount of things to say. The expanded character count simply meant we could say those things in fewer tweets.

I have relied heavily on linking my tweets and creating threads; users can read a well-thought-out idea as it developed in real time, and when I am done, they can share the thread with their followers, cosigning and endorsing the things I have written. It is also a way for me to respond to another tweet and add my own expanded commentary in the moment, without having to formulate a blog post and share it later on, after the moment passed. Twitter has been instrumental in altering how I share and consume information, which relies on influence, timeliness, and brevity. I think that is true for how others share and consume information, as well. If you're not addressing something *in the moment*, you're late, and if you're late, you have missed the window for an audience. As discouraging as that is for people who very much value writing out their ideas in cohesive bodies of work before they respond to the day's happenings, it is a reality to which we are all adapting. For Black women trying to educate as many people as possible about intersectionality in feminism, the deep impact of racism, the crippling of classism, and more, we have to meet people where they are, and Twitter, the platform that encourages brevity and speedy engagement, is where we find them.

One of my most popular threads presents the theory that "allies," as used in social justice circles focused on identity and anti-oppression work, do not exist. Written in August of 2015, it is still widely shared and has even been taught in high school and college courses, referenced in articles, and cited in presentations and panels about allyship, movements, and more.[7] My thesis asserts that, by definition, allies, when used in this realm as most people use the term, cannot exist, because alliances are formed to the mutual benefit of the joining parties. Since there is no mutual benefit for oppressors and privileged people when the oppressed are liberated, there can be no such alliance, thus no "allies." In my longest Twitter thread ever, I offered that people use the term "ally" as a catchall term and performative act to assure others that they aren't bad people. It was received well, for the most part, with many people, mostly White, saying that the thread helped them think differently about "allyship." Those who disagreed, in my opinion, did not like being stripped of a label they could wear to show people they were one of the good Whites. People get really upset when you tell them everything they've believed to be true is wrong or offensive, I have learned. I'm working on not being so entertained by their tantrums.

The original tweet has over 150,000 impressions and has been engaged by over 37,000 accounts, with several hundred retweets and even more "quoted tweets," signifying a shift in how tweets are shared. No longer do people have to retweet every single tweet to make sure their followers see an entire train of thought; they can either retweet the original tweet or they can quote the original tweet and add a short commentary like "Thread!" or "This thread is so important!" to encourage them to read the full chain of tweets. It has become a way that someone who is less knowledgeable about a particular topic or issue can share someone else's articulation of often complex and nuanced ideas with other people they believe can benefit from reading those tweets.

While people from all walks of life now use this method of tweeting, I believe it was popularized by Black women as a reflection of our natural conversational practices. Of course, I can't prove that people are threading tweets because they've been inspired by us. With what we know about how influential Black culture is, however, and how quickly people try to copy what we do to be "cool," I don't think my idea is too far off. It has become one of the ways those who have little or no access to mainstream media or the academy can share their thoughts and analyses on various issues relevant to their existence as Black women and be affirmed by other Black women participants who could acknowledge their thoughts and experiences as being valid and shared by others. Be they queer, disabled, older, plus-sized, darker-skinned, or any other identity that further marginalizes them beyond their Blackness, more Black women have been able to have their critical analyses of everything from Black feminist theory of the 1970s to hip-hop misogyny of the 1990s shared with people who would otherwise never have considered the things we're thinking about and sharing. Rather than speak over and for us, more people realize and understand the power of our voices and want to make sure others have access to our work, which is vital to the growth and spread of discourse and movements.

Our threads are often wrongly called "rants," which is problematic in that it connotes anger or forcefulness, a persistent stereotype about Black women. Too often, people have visceral reactions because they either feel attacked or excluded, and instead of pausing to process what they're reading, they chime in with commentary that is counterproductive or reductive. When people engage your tweets and threads in real time, as you're developing your sermon and receiving encouragement from your congregation, you have to be mindful that someone will try to derail your message with racist or sexist commentary, or some equally hateful contestation. And because Black women thrive in call-and-response dynamics, we find that many threads include addressing these attempts at derailment, which, ironically, strengthens the message by mitigating the hole-poking attempted by contentious users. Think of it, then, as a way to present critical analyses and engage in the debate and discussion of it without waiting for it to be published, read, and responded to weeks or months down the line. There is power in the ability to control the narrative in real time, and Black women have harnessed this power to shut down much of the opposition they face when simply trying to share their experiences as Black women in this world.

The Twitter thread, then, unveils Black women's processing of our own identity-shaping experiences, contextualizing our own understanding of ourselves as others watch and even participate in that process with either positive support or negative derailment. And as a pastor might shift her sermon based on how it engages the congregation and what responses it evokes, we might find ourselves taking our threads in different directions than we at first intended, and therein lies the beauty and power of it—our community-building through call-and-response discourse has created an environment for us to collaborate and work on collectively shaping new narratives for the world. Threads are primary resources that document how Black women's sociopolitical analysis, critical gender and race theories, and cultural commentary are often developed on the fly, in real time. Many of these threads are, in my opinion, as valuable as academic papers published in journals that relatively few people have access to, and the ways in which they influence and educate all those who engage and even participate in them cannot be understated.

Of course, communication involves more than just words. Whether we are giving looks, making faces, waving hands, rolling necks, sucking teeth, or chuckling, Black women communicate in unique ways that are often only understood by other Black women. We can have entire conversations without saying a word. It is no different on social media, where we often use emojis, pictures, and GIFs to convey our thoughts or to react to things we come across. We were among the earliest to use images in tweets that weren't sent to promote articles or share statistical data or similar information. Adding an expressive image to a tweet could turn it into a hilarious joke or dismiss someone else's nonsensical commentary. The extra punctuation of a well-placed still image or animated GIF reflects a certain swag that Black women have and are uniquely able to communicate online. As the use of these accents became more popular with Black Twitter users, of course others took notice and began to copy the style. And since most of the images being used were of Black women, we began to see a plethora of non-Black women and brands using these images for their own tweets, to convey their own emotions. Like the co-opting of "You go, girl!" by White women in the 1990s, this technique did not feel genuine coming from "others" and began to rub some people the wrong way. In a *Teen Vogue* article, Lauren Michele Jackson argues that the use of Black women's images and GIFs is a form of "digital blackface," wherein White social media users will pretend to be Black and adopt exaggerated, stereotypical names, words, and memes as a way to ridicule us. Jackson suggests that the use of Black women's imagery is a way to "blacken up" their presentation, usually to try to gain more attention or come off as "cool."[8] Black cool, particularly the swagger of Black women, is often co-opted by those who wish to appear more hip or culturally relevant, so it is no surprise that co-opting the use of memes, reaction pictures, and GIFs became the thing to do. We know that Black women's influence manifests in others finding value in things we would do naturally. That does not mean that people will avoid engaging in harmful adaptations of our behaviors, and to Jackson's point, the fact that people easily access these GIFs by typing in phrases like "sassy Black woman" or "angry Black woman" lets us know that while they continue to jack our style, they have little respect for us as cultural innovators and rely on misogynoir to be "cool."[9]

As stated earlier, Twitter's design is inherently call-and-response, which is commonly used in Black women's communication styles, particularly our conversational style. It makes sense, then, that as Twitter developed into more of a community space where people chat with each other in real time, we would begin to engage each other in more communal ways. Asking "Who is watching [whatever television show]?" was a call to congregate and share the experience of enjoying a television show together, despite being located in different homes, cities, states, and even countries. Blogger and podcaster Xavier D'Leau (@XavierDleau) is known for asking, "Are we watching [television show] as a family?" signaling it was time to get situated, turn on the television, and log on to join in the shared experience of watching and tweeting commentary. At first, it was popular mostly with major events like award shows and performance specials. Over time, this participatory viewing experience, called "live-tweeting," caught on and became a staple aspect of Black Twitter's community time. Watching a show and live-tweeting is simply a manifestation of that conversational call-and-response engagement between Black women and television and film and we popularized it through making plans to have live-tweeting watch nights or events that were promoted ahead of time as opposed to an impromptu congregation.

Ashlee Blackwell, founder of *Graveyard Sisters*, a blog with a niche focus on the presence of Black women in horror films, created #FridayNight-Horror, a monthly live-tweet event. Since 2013, she has created space for people to learn more about Black women's contributions to a cinematic genre in which we are severely underrepresented. Blackwell, who identifies as a feminist, was introduced to feminism by way of Black studies classes in college during which her professors noted Black women's critical contributions to feminist theory and the feminist movement. Africana Womanism was a central theme in many of her reading assignments and she began to identify as a feminist long before becoming involved with social media.

I found Blackwell because I'm a *huge* horror movie fan and one of her tweets was retweeted onto my timeline by Jamie Broadnax of the blog *Black Girl Nerds*. Tweeting under the name @GraveyardSister, Blackwell shares blog posts and articles highlighting Black women's role in horror movies, both on and behind the screens. I felt like I'd hit the jackpot and immediately subscribed to her blog, which has an average of a thousand daily views, and joined the ten thousand plus fans who follow her on Twitter. I had an opportunity to learn more about Blackwell and when I discovered that she identifies as a Black feminist, I wasn't surprised— we really do run everything. I asked her what inspired her to begin #FridayNightHorror and what she sees as the future of Graveyard Sisters. She answered in an email:

> Black Girl Nerds founder, Jamie Broadnax, and I spent one Friday night online bored and wanted to watch a film together along with others. I was to pick the movie and was in the mood to watch/monitor the reactions of others watching one of the most craziest, goriest, and very effective horror films I had seen recently. Jamie and I thought it so much fun that she encouraged me to do it more often. Then I thought more about how I even began loving horror so much and one of my origin stories is how Philly 57 had a Friday night movie on back in the late 1980's. Many times, it was a horror film. One that became a favorite of mine, A Nightmare on Elm Street 4: The Dream Master, is one I hotly anticipated almost every week. I wanted to bring that feeling back for myself or others once a month.
>
> I would like to see [Graveyard Sisters] as a part of horror studies curriculums in universities everywhere that study the work. I want Graveyard Shift Sisters [to] be a part of the new knowledge currently being developed by myself and others who focus on women of color in front and behind the screen in the horror genre.
>
> I learned the value of social media through Graveyard Shift Sisters. The first highlight has been how much feedback I have gotten, even within the first two months of launching the website, about the fact that I unknowingly filled a major gap in horror fandom, scholarship, and recognition. That has been the biggest reward for doing this and I appreciate how a truly diverse audience of people see the value in it. Another has been given paid opportunities to write for other major/horror outlets to expose the brand to even more audiences.[10]

While Blackwell has not been paid to tweet anything, her niche social media presence attracts the attention of celebrities who have starred in the movies being live-tweeted and discussed on her blog. For example, in 2014 Rachel True, a Black American actress who starred in *The Craft*, joined the live-tweet of the movie with the #FridayNightHorror hashtag, making the experience of live-tweeting the movie even more exciting.

Broadnax emerged early on as one of the most prominent figures in the live-tweeting sphere. The blog, founded in February of 2012 to represent and celebrate nerdy brown women, created a unique space centering and highlighting the interests and experiences of Black women who identified as nerds—they grew up being interested in things that were often dismissed or ridiculed as being "nerdy" or unpopular with the "cool kids." While Broadnax was not the first to gather together Black women from "nerd" or "geek" backgrounds and identities, she has been viewed by many as someone with undeniable influence in the mainstreaming of this long-marginalized demographic. What began as an organically formed community that simply enjoyed connecting with each other online and watching television shows and films together has grown into an enormously influential community that attracts and engages major Hollywood stars who are honored to be featured guests during live-tweeting events and who grant exclusive interviews to *Black Girl Nerds*. This community, which has relied on the content and labor of many underrepresented people and writers who have used the platform as a launchpad for their own writing and content-creating careers, became one of the most influential on social media and has been driven by the creativity and dedicated labor of Black women, many who identify as feminists.

I contacted Broadnax about *Black Girl Nerds*' origin story and her own growth as a social media influencer. "I honestly used the BGN account to watch the shows I liked and live-tweeted them . . . I just love how live-tweeting brings communities together," she shared with me and acknowledged, "Having a large influential following has made some impact on how those shows trend and are received on social media." But Broadnax insisted that she is just blogging for the love of it.[11] And though she'd embraced the principles of feminism prior to creating this platform, it was by being a voice for Black women in geek culture that she began to identify more as a feminist and include these principles into her platform.

*Black Girl Nerds* has featured several staff and guest writers, many of whom were being published online for the first time, and the content is as diverse as the community it represents. BGN launched a podcast in 2013, and both the blog and podcast regularly featured interviews with actors, authors, and filmmakers whose work represents the "nerd" identity. As their popularity increased and reach expanded, they attracted the attention of some major stars, including Oprah Winfrey, who in 2018 tweeted Broadnax, referencing a meeting between the two of them. Oprah. Mother Oprah, the Goddess of all things media, engaged Broadnax publicly on the social media space in which *she* held court.

Over the years, *Black Girl Nerds'* live-tweet events (yes, *events*) have drawn hundreds of participants, including people directly involved with the television show or film being live-tweeted. They made history in 2013 by live-tweeting Eddie Murphy's *Coming to America*, which ultimately trended, a first for any movie, particularly one that was nearly thirty years old. Using the hashtag #ComingToAmerica, BGN rallied fans and movie-watchers to load the film on Netflix or insert their own DVDs, press play when instructed to do so, and share their best talk-to-the-screen quips and witticisms with those watching along. This live-tweeting event set the bar, raising the standard for how Twitter users engage each other in shared experiences of watching television and films.

These events lead to trending hashtags and the shows being featured among the top trending topics on Twitter, which draws more attention to them. As exemplified with the increased popularity of live-tweeting, something that we do as a second-nature behavior has been turned into a key marketing tactic for major companies and not just for watching television. To keep us connected, we assign hashtags to these live-tweeting events, and when hashtags are "trending," they attract the attention of people from all over the social mediasphere. People then engage the trending topic mostly with curiosity and a desire to join in on the conversation. As trending is now included in assessments of a show's popularity, these events have increased viewership for television shows and have even helped a number of shows get renewed or brought back after being canceled.

When Black women create space, often a necessary response to perpetual exclusion and erasure, we create environments that are supportive, nurturing, and inviting even to people who do not identify as Black women. Not only do we create the engaging and collaborative communities, we decide what is "cool" and culturally relevant; participants often wait to take their cues from us and our actions. We innovate as they imitate and look for ways to turn a profit from our inventiveness. It was primarily Black feminist women who popularized this method of engaging entertainment, and in 2014, Forbes addressed the influence of live-tweeting events on viewership and engagement. "Programs whose cast members live-tweet when the show is airing generate 64% more discussion," wrote staff writer Jeff Bercovici, who looked at viewer conversion rates when actors participated in live-tweets versus when they did not.[12]

As live-tweeting increased in popularity, companies realized that this behavior boosted the exposure of these television shows and films to people who might not otherwise have been aware of them. This free advertisement was a marketing dream—people voluntarily promoted shows and encouraged people to watch them as part of a communal experience, and with each live-tweet the brand awareness grew. Advertisers did not have to pay a penny for it. And because we so looked forward to participating in these live-tweet events, it was a guaranteed effective marketing tactic. The only problem is that primarily Black women end up performing free labor simply by being ourselves, and that puts us at risk for exploitation, even by our own. While Broadnax did most of her live-tweeting for free, for the love of it, she became connected with a marketing company that compensated her for live-tweeting certain shows and she'd been able to earn revenue for BGN-related content and appearances.

For the most part, we have seen the evolution of this type of marketing and now, more and more Black women, feminists especially, are being compensated for using their platforms in these ways. When Black women used live-tweeting to garner support for Shonda Rhimes's hit show *Scandal*, BGN launched "Scandal Nights," a weekly live-tweeting event that played a major role in keeping the show in the top trending topics on Twitter and was credited with helping the show get renewed. (It would go on to have five more seasons.) This game changed completely! Kerry

Washington, *Scandal*'s star, regularly joined in the chats, and Rhimes followed the BGN Twitter account, retweeting several of the live-tweets from the show. After the historic *Coming to America* event and the support of *Scandal*, no longer could these live-tweet hashtags and conversations be ignored or dismissed as regular chatting. As noted by Jared Goldsmith, vice-president of marketing for NBC Digital, "live-tweeting is creating a shared experience where audiences can feel like they're on an extended couch." He also shared, on a panel during the 2014 Social Media Week, that "these shows have a way to connect with audiences like never before thanks to this technology."[13] Broadnax notes her first paid campaign was for *The Carmichael Show* on NBC, during which she live-tweeted the show and engaged a few of the actors, and the campaign performed so well that the show reached an all new audience and was renewed.

Having been paid to live-tweet all types of shows over the years, I realized early on that efforts to increase viewership made primarily by marketing agencies trying to promote White-led television shows did not jump off as well. Despite having a couple of influencers like me tweeting, the shows just did not catch on. The live-tweeting scripts they created and wanted us to adhere to simply did not translate into trending topics or boosts in viewership. They weren't organic enough and they had a lot of rules and restrictions on what we could tweet and not tweet. There remains no comparison to the ways in which Black people engage each other, particularly Black women. There is power in those hashtags, and now, because of years of unpaid efforts made by Black women, the live-tweeting events are more structured, coordinated often by production companies or television networks, and almost expected. We no longer have to ask if we're going to watch a show as a family because it is assumed that there will be some type of live-tweet happening. Finally, Black women with huge followings and social influence, who have been providing years of free marketing services, are being justifiably compensated for their labor. We changed the game, forever.

# CHAPTER 4

# The Influencers

---

@NICKIMINAJ . . . Black women influence pop culture so much, but are rarely rewarded for it.

6:14 PM—21 Jul 2015[1]

---

**OVER THE YEARS, I** have been approached by several brands, retailers, and television networks and film companies to support their marketing efforts. I may be asked to curate a live-tweet chat or event to build viewership for a television show or film, or to promote a product or service of some sort. My experience is not unique, by far, but it is interesting in the sense that I did not start out as, nor did I ever aspire to be, an "influencer" in this sense. Several of my peers have made an entire career out of these types of opportunities, and in recent years we have seen more focus paid to Black women with large followings whose influence can have direct impact on the purchasing and consumption decisions of their fans.

According to Influencer Marketing Hub, an online resource for all things related to influencer marketing, an influencer has the power to affect the purchasing decisions of others because of their authority, knowledge, position, or relationship with their audience. Influencers who focus on a particular niche are seen as go-to people in this area of expertise.[2] The most likely influencers are celebrities and athletes, but there is a growing need for bloggers and content creators—people who have long focused on specific issues and have amassed followings based on their expertise, insider access, and knowledge. Influencer marketing has exploded as agencies realize not only that it costs less to have a social media persona promote their product or service as virtual spokespersons, but they're able to reach demographics underserved by traditional marketing, often due to bias and shortsightedness on behalf of marketing executives. As is the case with Black women, marketing agencies have discovered the powerful influence we have in social media spaces and know they would be severely remiss in ignoring the growth potential in our market and with our audiences.

I began doing influencer advertisements when I was on the staff of BlogHer.com, a site geared toward female bloggers and content creators that officially merged with SheKnows.com in 2015. As the "Love & Sex" section editor, I grew my own personal following immensely in the three years I worked for the site; it was a treasure trove of subscribers looking for advice on how to find a man, keep a man, and knock his socks off in bed. My popularity as a sex-positive feminist blogger had attracted the site's senior editors to me, and when they offered me the opportunity to join the team, I jumped on it. There was an influencer program that allowed participants to sign up for various ad campaigns by brands like Walmart, Dove, and Coca-Cola, and we were paid based on the content we created to promote those products and services. We might be asked to share a set number of tweets or Facebook posts in a specific period of time, or attend focus group events and compose sponsored blog posts to share our experiences and promote products. For someone trying to make her way in the blogosphere, this was a pretty sweet deal, and I was happy to participate in what seemed like minimal work for a strong reward.

Though the appeal was strong, I did not accept every offer made to me, and I remain committed to upholding my own personal values in my endorsements of companies and services. I opted out of a lucrative opportunity to do promotion for Walmart because I took issue with what I believed to be Walmart's exploitative hold on American labor, wages, and overall health. Then, I did a campaign with Dove before realizing that it, too, as a subsidiary of Unilever, has been linked to practices I do not support. And when I realized that Unilever owned almost every product in my house, I started becoming more aware of how often we compromise our values for consumption habits, and I made a commitment to at least be mindful of this in evaluating my promotional opportunities and what products and services I was willing to endorse using my name and brand.

I knew that I was valuable as a Black woman in that space. BlogHer and SheKnows weren't known for being culturally diverse as far as writers were concerned. In fact, they were known mostly as hubs for White mommy bloggers whose lifestyle blogs showcased their bratty kids, inconsiderate husbands, and flavorless recipes. Women of color were there, of course, and I joined the editorial team with the hope of helping these outlets reach a broader, more diverse audience, not just culturally but with regard to religion and sexual identity and orientation as well. As I engaged more of the women sharing content with and producing content for these sites, either virtually or at annual conferences, I realized that not only were their casual lifestyle blogs lucrative but that some of these women were making thousands of dollars a month for product reviews and advertising—*thousands.* Every now and then, I'd encounter a unique blog that had a different angle with a niche audience, but for the most part, I did not find much of interest in the content they were producing, so I wondered how they'd been able to get these types of sponsors. And I wanted to know how I could get more Black women involved in this hustle—we deserved some of that money too!

BlogHer/SheKnows helped launch and further the careers of a number of Black women, though, and it is important to make note of this. Luvvie Ajayi, author and social commentator; Kathryn Finney, founder of digitalundivided; Majora Carter, founder of Sustainable South Bronx; A. V. Perkins, popular DIY blogger; and several others found immense support for and promotion of their work in this community, and they've each gone on to establish themselves as widely recognized experts and voices in various spaces. For a while, the best, if not only, way that a Black woman could earn money for her blog content, be it on traditional blogs or via microblogging on Twitter and Facebook, was through larger White-owned and operated networks like BlogHer/SheKnows, because those were the companies that attracted the brands willing to spend money on influencer marketing. By tapping into this market, Black women found themselves gaining exposure to markets and opportunities beyond communities like Black Twitter or their own blog subscribers (read: White people with White money). Not only could we get paid to promote products and services, we were being asked to do speaking engagements, sit on panels, do

TEDx- or TED-style talks, write and produce content for major publications with household names, and more.

*Ebony* magazine is one such household name. For decades, *Ebony* graced the coffee tables of Black homes and the racks in beauty salons and barbershops. I grew up reading *Ebony*, as it was one of the few resources that kept up with current events in Black communities, Black entertainment, business, health, beauty, fashion, and more. It was in *Ebony* that I could read more about my favorite artist's newest album and learn about important historical events. Unfortunately, like several other printed publications, the Johnson Publishing–owned *Ebony* and *Jet* magazines began to see a decline in readership and sales in the early 2000s. Part of the decline was recession-based, and even Condé Nast brands experienced declines. But a big part of it was that the content did not resonate with younger audiences who were driving the consumption of entertainment, beauty, and fashion news. These magazines were losing touch with their target demographic because as online publications and digital media were on the rise, they weren't keeping up with the relevant online content that continued to attract younger viewers and keep them coming back.

In 2012, Ebony.com relaunched with new management at the helm. Kierna Mayo, an award-winning journalist and cofounder of *Honey* magazine with roots deep in hip-hop culture journalism, came on as editor in chief and vice president of digital content. Jamilah Lemieux, a longtime blogger and content creator widely recognized as a modern Black feminist thought leader, also joined the team, eventually becoming the senior digital editor before she moved to the print magazine in 2015. Lemieux had a large following long before she began to work with Ebony.com, and it was that following and reach that helped propel Ebony.com to becoming the premier site for content catering to Black interests. Offering freelance opportunities to up-and-coming and established writers, Ebony.com, led by these dynamic Black feminist women, created space for bloggers, tweeters, content creators, and burgeoning journalists alike to be published with a reputable periodical and have their work shared with a large audience. Writing for Ebony.com made you "official" and served as a great résumé booster for anyone trying to make a mark as a social or political commentator, a reporter or journalist, or as a purveyor of pop culture.

It wasn't simply that the opportunities expanded for writers of color, it was that Mayo and Lemieux were especially committed to centering Black women's stories, amplifying their voices, celebrating their work, and honoring their beauty in ways that we had not previously seen in digital spaces. The duo reenergized the legacy of *Ebony* magazine by using digital space to reach a new audience. Their team pushed boundaries and challenged readers to think beyond the status quo. While they did feature pieces on pop culture, fashion, and other "clicky" content, they also delved into important, serious issues affecting the Black community and engaged people whose voices and stories would have otherwise gone unheard.

It was at Ebony.com that I wrote my very first column for a major publication. It was a sex column called #TalkLikeSex, named after a graphic rap song by the hip-hop artist Kool G Rap. I was definitely conflicted over the use of the song's title, because Kool G Rap was not only known for his blueprint lyricism; he was also accused of being an abuser of women. Famed author of *Confessions of a Video Vixen*, Karrine Steffans, alleged in the book that the rapper had physically and sexually abused her. Though she later confessed to fabricating some of her stories, the allegations of abuse lingered. The rapper's song was one that was not only graphic, but degrading in many ways, so for me, using the song title as the title for my column was a way of subverting his "talk" about sex—and other degrading depictions of sex and sexual abuse and disregard of women in hip-hop music—and changing the way we, Black women, particularly those raised on hip-hop culture, talk about sex. Working with editor Miles Marshall Lewis, a partnership made possible by Lemieux herself, I produced weekly content that addressed everything from polyamory to BDSM to "enthusiastic consent." Much of the content was influenced by and drawn from topics I'd written about on my blog or on Facebook and Twitter—only this time I was being paid for my content and it was exposed to a larger audience. The column helped me expand my reach and grow my audience, while helping a lot of people understand feminism, specifically sex-positive feminism, in a new way.

When Mayo and Lemieux moved to the print side of the publication, they continued to push the envelope as only Black feminist women can do. Their controversial cover story on the allegations of rape and sexual assault against Bill Cosby sparked heated, though much-needed, debate on the ways in which we condone or condemn Black men who are accused of harming women. Lemieux, never one to shy away from articulating raw honest truths and passionate opinions in defense of Black girls and women, would come under serious fire from all angles simply because she dared center the lives, stories, and concerns of Black girls and women. She fell under constant attack from everyone uncomfortable with a Black feminist woman unafraid to speak her mind across several platforms. Detractors accused her of selling out Black men and regularly attacked her with slurs and lies, despite the pieces that focused on racism, police brutality, and interviews, like the one I did with Samaria Rice, whose twelve-year-old son, Tamir Rice, was murdered by a Cleveland police officer in broad daylight at a park.[3] They made up stories to attack every angle of her life and made her the subject of vitriol that would shake even the strongest among us, yet she kept pushing and did not compromise on the important work she and the *Ebony* team were doing. And in April 2018, when Cosby was finally convicted of sexual assault, after decades of accusations and trials, the duo was vindicated in some way, having taken a progressive, public stance against him by way of the very publication that had celebrated him many times over his career.

During this same period of growth, other outlets like TheGriot.com, an NBC affiliate, HuffPost Black Voices, TheRoot.com, MadameNoire .com, NewsOne.com, Blavity.com, and Bossip.com emerged and rose in popularity for social media users looking for the latest information related to popular Black culture, politics, social justice, and enterprise. Well-established magazines like *Black Enterprise* also began to capitalize on the accessibility of an online audience. Many of these publications not only featured Black women as writers and editors, but were helmed by Black women. As social media has made our global Black Community feel smaller and more closely-knit, career opportunities for those of us who only dreamed about being published and read around the world increased. Several of the editors and contributors to these publications were talented Black women, a number of whom, like me, never had any formal journalism training; we simply had stories to tell, opinions to share, and a desire to help other Black women get "put on."

I left my column at Ebony.com after the company's response to the attacks on Lemieux from members of the Republican Party. In March 2014, Lemieux and Raffi Williams, a former deputy secretary for the RNC, became the center of a heated debate when Lemieux mistook Williams for a White man after he interjected into an online conversation she was having about Ben Carson's nonsensical something or other. She said, "Oh great, here comes the White dude telling me how to do this Black thing." Lemieux had no idea who Williams was. Based on his skin color and hair texture, he can be mistaken for White, but he identifies, as many other Black folks do, as African American. Of course the GOP jumped on this opportunity to criticize a Black woman, and Lemieux became embroiled in one of the nastiest, most disgusting displays of abusive misogynoir I have ever witnessed on social media. I started the hashtag #StandWith Jamilah because . . . what the fuck? Her @ replies were being filled with violence and hatred from White supremacists who were calling her all kinds of sexist and racist names. She was being accused of things so far removed from what she said, and it troubled me not only as a peer and Black feminist comrade, but as a human being. I wanted to show her that she was not alone in having to brave this storm and she wasn't. Scores of people joined in on the hashtag and began to show support for her and that they were in solidarity with her against the rabid attacks from the far right. When Reince Priebus, then chairman of the GOP, weighed in, all hell broke loose, so imagine my surprise when *Ebony* released a statement throwing Lemieux under the bus.

> As the magazine of record for the Black community, Lemieux's tweets in question do not represent our journalistic standard, tradition or practice of celebrating diverse Black thought . . . EBONY acknowledges Senior Editor Jamilah Lemieux's lack of judgment on her personal Twitter account and apologizes to Raffi Williams and the Black Republican community.[4]

I quit *Ebony* immediately. I did not want to continue to contribute my content and take money from a company that would not stand with its valued contributors and the main ones who helped them come back from the graveyard of irrelevance. I informed my editor that I would be ending my column and he was shocked, as I expected him to be. While the extra income was definitely helpful to a divorced mom on a social worker's salary, accepting their money did not feel right to me at the time. I would later contribute an article to Ebony.com for free, an interview with Tamir Rice's mother, Samaria, and I believed her need for broader exposure outweighed my silent protest. And when Lemieux and Mayo moved to the print side, I was asked to write a paid article on sex positivity and why we need it. Not wanting to pass up the opportunity to reach a different audience that might not be having the kinds of conversations about sex I believed we need to have, I agreed. (Full disclosure: I fell victim to the #EbonyOwes scandal, during which *Ebony* was accused and found guilty of not paying its contributors. It took me over five months to get paid, after getting major runaround, only to find out the magazine had been sold and was in transition and nearly bankrupt. I'm not saying karma is a bitch, but . . . maybe.)

Ebony.com *did* help a lot of us gain clout in the writing world and I became known as "*EBONY* contributor" when I was asked to speak at events or on news shows. The name carried weight and the seventy-year reputation could not be disputed, despite the challenges it went through after the GOP debacle. Another prominent Black magazine, *Essence*, also began to establish its online presence and expanded its reach by attracting many of the same writers who were once loyal to Ebony.com. When Chrissy Coleman, former senior culture and entertainment editor of *Essence*, approached me to write an article about the former NFL quarterback Colin Kaepernick, based on a Twitter thread I wrote about famous Black athletes who had faced racial discrimination, I jumped on it. What I, and others, began to realize is that so many editors and content curators began following those of us with high tweet engagement and some even began using our tweets as source material. Either they were taking the tweets and using them in their "articles," or they were taking the ideas and sometimes original theories and expanding on them for their own paid pieces. I remember seeing one article that had, no lie, four original lines of text; the rest was a well-curated stream of tweets from me and others. Mainstream publications found a gold mine when they began following Black women with high follower counts who were well-versed not only in popular culture current events, but were also strong writers who were proficient in social media-based discourse. As more Black publications began to establish their online presence and bring their websites into the future, Black writers and thinkers, many of whom are Black feminist women, began to find homes for their art and their wisdom—paid work showcased in *our* spaces.

Connecting with *Essence* allowed me to share another passion of mine—music writing. Since 2015, I have run a blog on Medium.com that focused solely on writing about Black women in music, be they writers, producers, rappers, or singers. I once had a dream of becoming an ethnomusicologist who would study women in hip-hop and focus on hip-hop's feminism. Since that dream was never realized, I found a new space to share my critical analyses of not only Black women's contributions to music but also the story behind the art they created. I wrote pieces about how Lil' Kim changed hip-hop music forever and how Missy Elliott was overlooked as a sexual being because she was plus-sized. I was able to explore nuances and backstories as I educated people about rather little-known facts about some of their favorite artists. I did all of this unpaid because it allowed me to maintain my creativity without feeling like I was laboring. The more pieces I wrote for publications like *Ebony*, *Time*, or the *New York Times*, the more I began to feel like my writing was getting away from me and becoming more like work. The *Medium* blog allowed me the chance to go back to the writing that I loved, the passionate work that spoke from my soul. After a year of maintaining this blog, I got the opportunity to write a music piece for *Essence* that would lead to regular music writing—album reviews, historical narratives, eulogies . . . I became one of the primary music contributors at Essence.com. My focus remained primarily on Black women in music and how feminism reveals itself in musical content, but I was also able to share my passion for hip-hop music and culture and cover some of my favorite artists like A Tribe Called Quest and Prodigy of Mobb Deep.

Another sista who proved how social media can launch a career is Angela "The Kitchenista" Davis, a self-taught chef who has built her career primarily by sharing her talents online. I encountered her on Twitter and was immediately drawn to her because we share the same birthday. Her food always looked delicious and I had hopes that she would start charging people for the recipes. Listen, ask anyone who knows me . . . I am always looking for a way to monetize talents. She did not disappoint and over six years, her blog, *The Kitchenista Diaries*, became one of the most popular food blogs online. I interviewed her, via email, to get a better understanding of how she was able to leverage social media to build her successful personal cheffing business and garner brand ambassador deals and endorsements, including a commercial spot with Aveeno.

**FEMINISTA JONES:** When did a major brand first approach you about a collaboration?

**ANGELA DAVIS:** My first influencer opportunities came from Johnsonville Sausage, about two years after I launched. I did a series of blog recipes using their products. Looking back is kind of painful because I took on some of those early gigs for essentially what amounted to the cost of ingredients.

**FJ:** How did the Aveeno ad come to be?

**AD:** Social media exposure and word-of-mouth led me to be recommended behind the scenes to be the talent for Aveeno's commercial. A Black woman working for the local production company here in D.C. was familiar with my work. She threw my name into the mix when she saw it could be an opportunity to work with me, even though it wasn't directly related to food. The commercial was in partnership with TV-One, so they were specifically looking for talent from that demographic. When she called me about the commercial I accepted the same day. I was terrified at the thought of being on TV but it was just one of those things you don't turn down.

**FJ:** What role has social media played in your ability to grow your business and get exposure?

**AD:** Social media was an integral part of my brand from the beginning. All of my content was digital and thus relied on social media shares to gain any kind of traction and recognition. It wasn't until a few years in that I started generating business offline, such as catering,

but even those jobs have all been referrals from within my social
media network—I have not yet paid for traditional advertising. My
public dinner events, from the beginning, were planned around using social media to sell tickets, create a buzz during the events with
live tweets and photos, and to create a space for my guests to meet
others from our social media community in person.

**FJ:** Any highlights of your career so far that happened as a direct result
of your social media exposure?

**AD:** Cooking for The Roots (a hip-hop group) was a surreal experience. It came about because Black Thought [the lead MC] had
followed me for a while on Twitter and heard about my sweet
potato pies. He tried to arrange for some pies to be delivered to his
assistant, but when that became too complicated he suggested I get
in touch with his manager about catering their next concert in the
city. I didn't set out to be a celebrity chef, but social media exposure has created some cool perks along the way.

I share all of this as examples of how Black women have been able
to leverage social media to become influential thought leaders, respected
artists, and go-to cultural critics and content creators. For too long, the
music industry has shown preference to male writers and when it comes
to hip-hop, few people can even name five prominent female writers who
have made a name covering the culture's art. For too long, periodicals
have favored the voices of White men over everyone else, so to be able to
publish in the *Washington Post* and *Time* is a pretty big deal for someone
with no formal journalism education or experience. Whereas much of
our critical theory work has been buried in niche publications or archived
in the annals of history, with the exception of a few heroines like Angela
Davis and bell hooks, social media has created a pathway for greater exposure for our voices. We have, in many ways, been able to circumvent the
traditional academic and journalistic tracts to find ourselves and our work
front and center, more accessible not only to the targeted audiences of
these outlets, but to those who have traditionally been excluded from exposure to this kind of thought and discourse. Racism and sexism have long
edged Black women to the margins of the academy and have limited the

opportunities for journalistic prestige, but in social media spaces, we have been able to have our voices and stories amplified in ways never imagined.

In this same vein, another prominent group powerfully emerged as representatives of a demographic living under the perpetual threat not only of systemic oppression, but actual death: Black trans women. Despite being raised by a queer Black woman and identifying as one myself, I grew up with what I now understand as horribly transphobic notions and stereotypes. I open with this not seeking empathy or understanding about some transformation—no. I say this because it is a past version of myself that I own and while I disavow it, I have spent more years thinking negatively about transgender people than I have affirming them. Even in my earlier days on social media, I often used the "t-word" slur and degrading words like "shim" or referring to a trans person as an "it." I once read someone say that there is no excuse for previous transphobia, and I agree. However, it was not until I was on Twitter that I even learned what "transphobia" was.[5] I had never heard of the term before and when I began to listen to trans women, I began to learn so much more about their experiences and the horrors Black trans women, especially, endure as they navigate the world with targets on their backs drawn primarily by Black, cisgender, heterosexual men. Dozens of trans people have been killed each year in recent years, with the underreported numbers on the rise across the nation. Part of the reason for the underreporting is because law enforcement, witnesses, families, and the media often misgender trans people, so the accuracy of the death toll is an estimation and will continue to be until society radically improves its acknowledgement and affirmation of trans identities.[6] After listening and learning, I rebuked my past commentary and committed to doing better, and I owe a great debt to all the trans women who have so openly and willingly shared their stories and strength with those of us who needed to wake up and end our bias and bigotry. I am by no means perfect, which is why I was initially hesitant to write about Black trans women extensively; I have learned the value of amplifying the voices of those even further marginalized than I am and not claiming any expertise on the lives of others. But how could I write a book about Black Feminism without including the Black women who need affirmation and support now, more than ever? I am grateful to them and their #GirlsLikeUs influence, not only on entertainment, as seen with La-verne Cox and her skyrocketing career, but also in popular culture, news, and politics with media maven Janet Mock; in business and tech with entrepreneur and actress Angelica Ross; dominating as a YouTube influ-encer like Kat Blaque; and forging forward with trans-affirming activism like Monica Roberts and Reina Gossett.[7] As trans visibility increases, and trans women are given more respect, love, encouragement, and support from within our community, the more trans women can contribute to the canon of Black womanhood. Trans women are women. Period.

Washington, DC, has the largest population of transgender people in the nation, with 2.33 percent of the population identifying as trans.[8] It was there that I discovered Dr. Lourdes Ashley Hunter. Well, I found her online, but she lived and worked in DC as founder and executive director of Trans Women of Color Collective when I first came across news of her work on Twitter. While investigating the meaning of the hashtag she used, #TWOCC, I found the collective, "a grass-roots funded global initiative created to offer opportunities for trans people of color, [their] families and [their] comrades to engage in healing, foster kinship, and build commu-nity."[9] When I was planning the Women's Freedom Conference of 2015, I wanted to center the voices of women of color around the globe, and when our team was looking for a keynote speaker, I knew I wanted us to feature a Black trans woman. Dr. Hunter was the first choice because of her work, her fortitude, and her grace. Having connected with her on Twitter and Facebook, I gained access to the spaces in which she held court, regularly calling out atrocities against trans people while representing her accom-plishments and those of other women like her. Dr. Hunter regularly posts images and videos of trans women of color experiencing joy, happiness, and celebrating their accomplishments, which is a defiant rebellion against the violence trans women continue to experience. In their joy, they affirm not only their humanity but their right to exist as free, happy people in a world that does little to protect their rights as human beings. Dr. Hunter graciously accepted the invitation, and delivered an incredibly powerful keynote speech during which she adamantly declared that trans women of color are facing the biggest threats to their health and well-being and that our feminist praxis must be intersectional and include trans women.[10]

I was honored to be able to center a Black trans woman's voice, but even more, I was able to share her words and her work with people around the world who did not know who she was prior to that conference. Did it make up for all the years I spent being a transphobe? No, and I was not looking for forgiveness or redemption. I was, at the very least, able to use my platform to boost another Black woman's work. That she was a trans woman was dope, though.

Imagine if Audre Lorde had access to Twitter in the 1970s and could share her now-famous and revered quotations in real time—what might that have done for the Black feminist movement of the time? If Angela Davis's speeches of the 1970s could be broadcast via Periscope and seen by tens of thousands a mere forty-eight hours after she delivered them? Imagine if Marsha P. Johnson could have shared video from the Stonewall riots the way Johnetta Elzie shared videos from Ferguson. Where might Black women be today, in our fight for equality and liberation, if these iconic thought leaders, artists, and activists were influencers in the way we understand them to be in our time? As we continue to carry the torches of the fires they lit decades ago, and reach more people through our influence, personal branding, activism, and innovative marketing strategies, we recognize the power we have and that is global reach, direct impact, and the ability to educate hundreds of thousands in minutes.

CHAPTER 5

# Talk Like Sex

**WHEN PEOPLE HEAR THE WORD** "feminist," they formulate all types of assumptions, judgments, accusations, and perceptions (mostly negative). "Man-hater," "ball-breaker," "bitch," "too aggressive," "sexually prudish" are just some that currently come to mind. Unfortunately, the prevailing perception of feminists is the stereotypical radical, single White lesbian in her forties who wants to burn every bra ever made. I'm not in any way saying there is anything wrong with that woman, but she does not represent even the slightest minority of self-proclaimed feminist women. When I began my blog, my goal was to try to change the perception of feminists, and with my tweets, blog, articles, videos, interviews, and speeches, I believe that I have at least gotten people to rethink all the negative stereotypes they've had about feminist women.

I have gotten positive feedback from many of my readers who say that I have given them a well-articulated voice in the feminist arena or that I have changed their minds about how they thought about feminism. At first, I loved that I could do that, and even now I try my best to expand folks' minds when it comes to understanding why feminism is essential to our collective growth in society. However, I began to resent it over time because I found myself complicit in trying to "soften" the image of feminism to make it more palatable for men and for women who do not identify as feminists. I tried to meet people where they were, which is a tactic I learned in my career as a harm-reductionist social worker. I told myself that if I could change a few minds, I could reduce the potential for violence against women and maybe make way for the next generation to be more enlightened and less patriarchal. But why was I acquiescing to their ignorance? Why was I trying so hard to make feminism appealing? I had internalized a lot of the negativity around feminism, and in many ways I was seeking acceptance as an "out" feminist. It was quite personal, and I was still working to reconcile my own connection to feminism and how it manifested in my life, influenced my worldview, and shaped my paradigm. Simply put, I did not want anyone calling *me* a hairy-armed, man-hating lesbian who fought to hold open her own doors. I had a lot to learn, and I like to think that I have, thanks to my exposure to other Black feminist women and more high-level discourse on feminist theory. But I knew one surefire, foolproof way to get people to pay attention—I decided to talk about my favorite subject: sex.

Some people, men, especially, refuse to accept that feminism is not about hating men or trying to be the dominant person in the relationship. I found it hard to believe anyone could think that of me, especially not anyone who has read my book *Push the Button*, or any of my other writings about BDSM, the acronym used to describe a lifestyle that supports indulgence in kinky activities involving bondage, discipline, and sadomasochism. I have written quite a bit about the intersection of feminism and BDSM. I have given lectures and talks on how feminism demands that women be able to make the best choices for their own bodies and, as such, that making an informed decision to participate in the BDSM lifestyle aligns with feminist theory. I have made no apologies for it, even when people have challenged me, suggesting BDSM is contradictory or not consistent with "real" feminism. My response to that is that since we cannot singularly define femininity or womanhood, or even masculinity or manhood, objectively, it is difficult to assign any one ideology as definitive "real feminism." As confusing as it may seem for some, the notion that it all boils down to individual paradigms is rather simple. Some argue that "feminist" has become a catchall label to explain away or excuse certain unbecoming behaviors that women choose to engage in (★whispers★ *sex*). That type of oversimplified accusation is, I believe, yet another way to shame and suppress the voices of people we ought to be listening to more: women.

Sex-positive feminism is a movement that began to gather steam in the 1980s on the heels of reproductive rights and economic justice feminist work of the late 1960s and 1970s. It grew into a movement that now offers sanctuary for those who believe sexual liberation is the key to women's liberation and that sex and sexuality have been weaponized against women as a method of controlling women's bodies. Rooted in the broader sex-positive movement, which affirms sexual freedom and sexual expression, regardless of gender identity, sexual orientation, race, class, or ability, sex-positive feminism centers the experiences of women who have historically been on the receiving end of negative sexual engagement and attitudes. Sex-positive feminists are generally supportive of sex work and sex-workers' rights, BDSM and kink, and polyamory, and we encourage public discourse and radical work to move forward in our progress toward achieving a sexually liberated society. Basically, many of us love fucking (or not fucking) and we believe that people should have freedom of choice, whether they identify as asexual or pansexual, choose to abstain or be celibate, or are people who simply want to engage in safe, healthy, harmless sexual activities—people should be able to do so without stigma, shame, or legislation denying them access to being their whole selves.

Are there limitations? Of course. We do not always agree on what those limitations are or where the lines should be drawn, and as within any "movement," there are factions leaning one way and factions leaning the other. Not every person who claims to be a sex-positive feminist supports sex workers who fight for decriminalization of sex work, for example, and while it makes no sense to *me*, I have encountered a few people who think that decriminalization will have a snowball effect leading to the decriminalization of harmful practices (like abuses against children). There are also some so-called sex-positive feminists who are trans-exclusive, or TERFS (trans-exclusive radical feminists), who do not support the inclusion of trans women in feminist movements. Again, pretty nonsensical in my view, but I am trying to keep it honest and let you hear both sides. These are two fringe examples, but there are more nuanced arguments within the sex-positive feminist movement about what makes sexual behaviors feminist and how participation in some activities is inherently antifeminist. My own thoughts about certain things have changed or evolved over time, so

I cannot so easily dismiss these nuances and arguments as being petty, contrarian points of view; I recognize that with time, education, experience, and personal growth, one's point of view can change and one's philosophical approach can evolve into something different than it was a decade ago.

There are two areas I believe are worth exploring more when it comes to sex-positive feminism, particularly Black women's connection to and involvement with it: engagement in BDSM/kink and diversity in racial representation to the public and within the movement. These are two areas in which I have significant expertise, and it is partly why, when I emerged as "Feminista Jones," I focused more specifically on Black women's sexual experiences and, even further, on our participation in the BDSM lifestyle. I recognized that there was little representation of Black women in public spaces designed to promote sex-positivity, and there was even less representation of Black people in preeminent BDSM culture, literature, art, and films. I wanted to do something about that. I can also admit that it was perhaps a bit of a selfish endeavor, as I was still working through my own decolonization and unlearning of harmful sex-negative ideas. For me, it was a way to not only find a safe space to learn and grow, but to explore my own wants and needs, and reclaim control of my body and develop a stronger, more positive connection to my own sexuality. It took me many years to begin to reconcile my experiences as a victim of multiple sexual violations, beginning at age four, and being involved in the BDSM community made me feel safe about exploring alternative means of healing, while also helping me work through lingering feelings of victimization. Writing the book was another step toward healing. It was also a small way to represent for Black women, whose historical connection to sexual discourse and activity has been tarnished by abusive misogynoir and by spiritual beliefs and religious dogma that condemns them for any sexual proclivities. If I could be a louder voice and take most of the pushback that I knew would come from speaking out, perhaps I could help blaze another trail for Black women trying to find their sexual selves.

And, well, I like to fuck. So there's that.

"Knob-slobbing feminism" became my entryway into that space, and was yet another one of my ventures that began one night on Twitter. It was 2010, and I started riffing on my Twitter page, probably in response to some fool saying something stupid about women and sex and feminism. This happened so often that I cannot recall the specifics of who said what, but you can pick any day ending in "y" on Twitter and find someone spewing ignorance. With my tongue deeply nestled in my cheek, I began tweeting about how women should feel comfortable in their enjoyment of sex and pleasing their men, and that doing so does not make one any less a feminist. I used the hashtag #KSFem for short and encouraged people to weigh in with their own thoughts. Thinking back on it, it was a funny night, and I had no idea that it would morph into anything serious. Still, having learned from others further along in their creative careers the importance of locking down social media spaces that have potential, I immediately created the blog site *Knob-Slobbing Feminism*, just in case, and eventually began regularly blogging under that tag about all things related to sex, sexuality, dating, relationships, and sexual health.

It was on this blog that I began taking anonymous questions from readers and followers, answering them in my blogs, and signing off as "Feminista Jones." It was another year or two before I changed my Twitter name to Feminista Jones from my original handle, @PurplePeace79. As FJ, I really enjoyed giving people some blunt, real-talk advice to help them solve their problems, and the blogs were being read and shared by people who would report back that my words helped them work through things in their own lives. I knew I was onto something, and I was gaining more attention, which was exciting. I began to draw the attention of folks who were more well-known than I was and even people who wanted me to come speak about sex and kink and feminism at conferences and write about it in their online publications. Interestingly enough, I changed the name of my site to FeministaJones.com riiight before Melissa Harris-Perry featured my video about mental health on her weekend MSNBC news, culture, and politics show. Imagine her having to say, "Feminista Jones, who blogs at *Knob-Slobbing Feminism*," on air. It would have been a win for our community, but it was at that moment that I realized what I wanted to do was broader, not limited to sex and sexuality, despite being lauded as an expert in that area.

Looking back on it, I laugh and cringe sometimes at some of my early work, because the quality of the writing leaves a lot to be desired, and in some pieces, I can see where I was holding on to some rather foolish ideas, including the need to pander to men to receive serious consideration. Silly me. Luckily, I grew up, learned more, and began to focus less on proving that women could be both feminist and suck dick, and that we could focus more on the historical implications of Black women's assertion of sexual liberation, the modern barriers to Black women's sexual freedom, and how we can and should work to bring about radical sociopolitical change for *all* women by centering sexual liberation in our discourse. I had long been active in other social justice spaces, as both an activist and social worker, so I began to bring all of those parts of me to the blog and to my other writing, which was increasing as my popularity grew.

By spring 2013, I had a column on Ebony.com and was the Love & Sex section editor at BlogHer.com, all based on the work and writing I had done on my own site and the support I had garnered from fiercely loyal fans and avid readers. What I was able to do was put a bold and proud Black face on the sex-positive movement, a movement that had been predominantly and rather starkly White for decades, with sprinkles of color here and there, and introduce sex-positivity to a community that had little understanding of or exposure to it as an ideology. I would like to think that through my visibility, advocacy, writing, speaking, and public support of other Black women doing sexy things, I have been able to move the needle and make the sex-positive space more diverse and inclusive of Black people, Black women in particular.[1]

As Black women try to navigate being hypersexualized *and* portrayed as exhibiting no sexual or romantic inclinations at all (see: "Mammy" or the "never-has-a-sex-life-or-any-existence-outside-of-being-the-Black-BFF-to-the-White-woman-on-a-soul-searching-journey"), the struggle to define oneself or align oneself with any ideology is real. When you add racism, sexism, classism, ableism, and such to the mix, it makes sense that Black women would shy away from openly claiming an identity that is regularly attacked and ridiculed, as if we do not already experience that just by being Black women. And if "feminist" continues to be a heavily burdened label even for White women to bear, adding "sex-positive" to it further complicates things and for Black women, it often means something different. I took this on as a personal mission and, to this day, continue to advocate for Black women's sexual freedom and liberation.

What troubles me is seeing younger sistas internalize harmful ideas about sex that I once held and have since grown out of. I see myself in them, and I reflect back on the ways in which believing ideas like women are less valuable the more sexual partners they have had or women should always be willing to pleasure their male partners led me to engage in reckless and occasionally dangerous activities. I extend some grace because of that and when I am able, I try to share some things I have written or some thoughts I have on a particular topic to try to help them think about it differently. I deeply entrenched myself in feminist scholarship and I share what I have learned and how my own sexual evolution has greatly improved my life, but I recognize that sometimes, people have to learn things on their own, even if it is the hard way.

I really began to think about the roots of what can be described as a disjointed connection to sex, and I directed my focus on the antebellum experiences of enslaved Black people. Though American slavery has been researched and written about extensively, I struggled to find a lot of resources on the sexuality and sex lives of enslaved people that did not center rape and exploitation or mention sex as part of a discourse on breeding. There is a solid body of literature that speaks to the weaponization of rape to subjugate enslaved Black women and reiterate Black men's inferiority to White men, as well as to how the laws institutionalized the rape of Black women in a sexual economy.[2] While insightful and valuable as we try to gain better understanding of sexual experiences, this scholarship mostly approaches sex as an oppressive act against the bodies of the enslaved, primarily enslaved women.

In 2012, Dr. Stacey Patton published "Who's Afraid of Black Sexuality?," an essay that presents the idea that Black scholars, or Blackademics, avoid the topic of Black sexuality; this resonated with me. In the piece, Patton explores how scholars have remained silent, in part, because of the fear that discourse around Black sexuality would derail their careers and that what we present about our sexually is based on White scholarly understanding and assessment of our experiences with sexuality.[3] And since

Black people have been historically severely underrepresented in clinical sex and sexuality studies, we don't really have much data to draw from to even begin to have conversations about how we participate in sex. Simply put, historians and scientists have not considered and explored Black sexuality as importantly as it should be considered, and as Patton suggests, "History without sexuality is incomplete." Since there is not as much available about the sex lives of enslaved Black people through even the early to mid-twentieth century as one might hope for, we have a great deal of our history missing because of the lack of documentation, testimonies, photographs, paintings, and scientific studies. Even when we read the narratives of formerly enslaved people, whether it is because of the interviewer's questioning or choices in recording, deeply held religious beliefs, or lingering feelings of shame, we do not encounter many testimonies specifically about positive experiences with sex.

Luckily, as Patton also noted, we have seen a significant increase in scholarship around Black sexuality in the last decade or so, with articles, books, workshops, panels, and conferences emerging that specifically center the Black experience with sex and sexuality. Even better, a good portion of it focuses on queer identities and experiences at the intersection of Blackness and queerness. Widener University in Pennsylvania, for example, has a robust graduate program in sexuality studies that has produced Black scholars who focus primarily on Black sexuality. Dr. Tracie Gilbert, who developed the theory of Black sexual epistemology, focuses on underlying social construction of racialized sexuality among African American and other diasporic communities. In her research, she connected with participants by using social media as a primary way to access as diverse a group as possible and survey them about their conceptualizations of sexuality. We spoke about the lack of positive representations and explorations of Blackness in sexuality studies, and she says the field of sexuality studies

> was never meant to study Black sexuality from a normative perspective, because it was built on inherently problematizing what we do. As a result, I think we've entered the field with the intention to solve our "problems" (i.e., unwanted pregnancy, degeneracy, and HIV/AIDS) or defending ourselves from the real problem of White supremacy. Black

sexologists, educators, and counselors have been so caught up with addressing racism in our field that we're only just now getting to the place of considering new ideas.[4]

Citing racism as the primary detractor, Gilbert notes that Black scholars are more readily willing to confront internalized White supremacy and anti-Blackness in the field and in themselves, and that there needs to be a stronger push to call into question the ontological foundation of sexuality studies itself.

An important point to note, as we see an emergence of public discourse around Black sexuality, is that a significant portion of it comes not directly from the academy, but from thinkers who exist outside of the academy (like me). There is something to be said about how we learn about and experience sexuality, and how we process our observations of Black sexuality's portrayal and representation in popular cultural media, art, and other nonacademic sources. Twitter, for example, is often the medium by which Black people discuss their thoughts on sex and sexuality, and others weigh in with either supportive or contrary opinions. These debates reveal a lot about how Black people learned about everything from their own anatomy to the "rules" by which they believe they are expected to live and behave when it comes to sex. And, as to be expected, many of these debates either start out with questions that position women as being of questionable value based on engaging in *any* sexual activity or quickly spiral into a complete cesspool of ignorance, crunchy sock wisdom, and YouTube University "facts."

We, as a people, continue to struggle with even talking about sex in the most basic terms, and it remains incredibly detrimental to our overall progress toward liberation. As a people whose bodies have been controlled for centuries, we still find it difficult not only to formulate our own ideas about how our bodies experience sex and pleasure, but also how to avoid making judgments about other Black people's sexual behavior based on our sex-negative socialization. Colonization appears to be at the root of our sexual disconnect, and we have a lot of work to do to decolonize our minds and liberate our bodies.

In another discussion about the sexual experiences of enslaved people, I had a great conversation with a group of people with whom I had gone to see the 2013 film *12 Years a Slave*, including Dr. Jamall Andrew Calloway, who has a PhD in systematic theology from Union Theological Seminary. Our immediate reactions were varied, as the movie was intense and brutal in its depictions of how enslaved people were treated, but we still tried to wrap our minds around everything portrayed in the film. The lively conversation turned toward the portrayal of sex in the film, and Dr. Calloway shared with me, as I wrote in an article for Ebony.com:

> Since slavery, the Black body has been sexualized almost exclusively from the perspective of and benefit to the White gaze, but the woman in the opening scene resisted and defied. She resisted the temptation of completely eradicating her sexuality from herself, even though it was a site of violence, of trauma. She defied the notion that her body was only property by demanding pleasure from another Black body on her own terms. I argue that by reclaiming and owning her sexuality in that small moment was ultimately her reclaiming her humanity.[5]

The theme of Black people owning sexuality on our own terms has become a guiding notion in my work in the sex-positive movement. I found that the reclamation of my body after sexual assault relied on my own positive affirmations and experiences with touch and sex. I began to take a more aggressive approach to sexual self-empowerment and decided to be vocal and public about my own experiences with sex, good and bad, my preferences, my sexual identity, even weighing in on social media conversations about sex. I eventually stopped participating in the latter because . . . what a waste of time, my goodness! My time is better spent speaking to and with more diverse audiences and like-minded individuals who are interested in hearing new or different perspectives on how others engage in sex and connect with their own sexual identities.

Speaking at sexuality conferences and on panels, making YouTube videos about sex-related matters, and writing articles, essays, and even a book became my go-to methods of spreading a message about sex-positive feminism and Blackness. Honestly, it's been a great deal of fun and I have learned so much from my peers, of all races, so I cannot imagine walking away from this type of work anytime soon. In 2014, I was asked to speak at SEXx, a conference presented by the Philadelphia-based group SEXx Interactive (which I officially joined in 2017 after moving to Philadelphia). I spoke about Black women's historical experiences with sex and sexuality, and that presentation motivated me to dig deeper and explore more about sexual trauma and methods of healing. As a trauma-informed mental health social worker, I strongly believe in healing and recovery, and I began thinking heavily about the connection between BDSM and sexual trauma. I started with myself after it dawned on me that, while engaging in some BDSM activities, I was being triggered, causing memories of terrible experiences to resurface. Something about the extreme nature of the activities was having a deep psychological effect on me, and it became difficult to ignore what I was experiencing; I decided to confront it instead. This was a period of struggle for me, as I worked to reconcile my willing participation in activities that involved voluntary use of whips and chains with being a Black female descendant of enslaved Black people in the Americas; how can any Black person be turned on by being fastened in chain-linked cuffs and flogged with leather straps? It took me some time to accept that my freedom involved my being able to make these specific choices for what happens to my body, but when I did, I felt stronger and more in control, even as I surrendered control to someone else.

What I realized is that for me, and possibly for others, engaging in BDSM activities can be a therapeutic approach to healing from sexual trauma, so my hope is to be able to find the resources and institutional support to study more about this. My hypothesis is that because engagement in healthy, safe, and consensual BDSM activities requires, among other things, a great deal of trust, endurance, and confrontation of one's own fears, people who have experienced sexual trauma can find ways to reclaim control of their physical and sexual experiences, confront and resolve their trauma-driven fears, and find sexual empowerment through structured, prescriptive engagement in BDSM. And since there is a growing number of sex-positive, kink-affirming mental health professionals providing therapy and treatment that is affordable and accessible, I am interested in seeing if there is any merit in developing treatment plans that include exploring how participation in BDSM can aid in recovery from sexual trauma.

Another thing I have thought long about, and shared my initial thoughts on, is how "hos" and "sluts" do not exist. "Hos don't exist" has been, for a few years, a refrain I have popped into those sexual debates I now generally avoid. A "ho" or "slut" is almost always a woman who has engaged in sexual behavior deemed inappropriate and damaging to her reputation. "Inappropriate" can mean anything, like having had sex with more than two men in her entire life, enjoying group sex with multiple men, or having the audacity to actually enjoy the sex she has and want to tell people about it. "Inappropriate" is left up to the people casting the judgment, making it completely arbitrary, yet some people actually think there is some universal understanding of what it means to be a "ho" or a "slut." The ways in which people respond to the idea is telling—most people do not want to eliminate the existence of a "ho" or a "slut" because they will no longer have anyone to degrade as a means of establishing a hierarchy that exalts them higher. If there is no "ho," there is no "At least I'm not a ho!" or "These hos out here be ['trippin',' 'crazy,' or insert your own derogatory adjective]." In a patriarchal society that values women primarily for the ways in which their bodies can be of use to men, competition is encouraged and women who internalize misogyny will happily jump into the arena with clear-heeled gladiator sandals.

In 2014, I wrote a piece for Ebony.com, "Deconstructing 'Ho,'" in which I attempted to break down the definition and historical uses of the word, the sexism in how it's used, and why it says more about the people who use it than the ones they use it against. A derivative of "whore," "ho" was first used in the 1960s by pimps who controlled the work and wallets of women who sold sex. Since we devalue sex work and dismiss the humanity of sex workers, using "ho" becomes a point of comparison; essentially, we are accepting that being a sex worker is a bad thing and any woman who behaves in the ways we ascribe to sex workers will be compared to them and labeled a "ho." For most people who use it today, it is not that deep, but that is because language is learned without much consideration for the origins. The subjective variations in definitions of the word "ho" are more than enough to call for an end to using it so broadly, and people sound ridiculous when they try to explain that "ho" is anything other than an idea created to relegate sexually active women to inferior status than everyone else. I wrote:

> The word is largely rooted in the idea that women are expected to be-
> have in sexual ways that are considered "appropriate" for women. It
> relies on the belief that women should remain as sexually inactive as
> possible. The construction of the "ho" concept gives men the power to
> decide a woman's value based on her sexual history. It also almost always
> relies on double standards about men's and women's behaviors, because
> many of the people calling women ho(e)s are doing a lot of the same
> things they accuse women of doing. There's nothing remotely fair about
> holding women to sexual standards that men aren't held to. Yet this ap-
> proach is so pervasive that even women hurl the label at each other, often
> in attempts to look better than other women.[6]

Nearly every time I tweet "Hos don't exist," someone responds saying that they do and if I bother to push them on it, their explanations are corny attempts at trying to sound smart. They simply cannot accept that they have no right to cast judgment on someone else's sexual behavior, and the fact that I attempt to strip them of that power rattles them. I am calling for an entire paradigm shift in which we stop assigning women value based on their sexual activity and we stop suggesting that there are universally accepted appropriate and consensual behaviors for anyone. That is diffi-cult for many people to accept since the idea of the "ho" or "slut" is so pervasive. I even challenged the use of the term "slut-shaming," because if we apply the logic of the phrase, comparing it to victim shaming or fat shaming, we ultimately accept that a "slut" exists and that women are being shamed for being "sluts." The truth is that they are shamed for be-ing sexually active in ways that other people deem inappropriate, so they are being sex-shamed or woman-shamed (because men are almost never referred to as "sluts"). This has also been controversial, as it challenges an entire feminist movement against "slut-shaming" to change its approach, and people are not ready to make the change, even when they accept the validity of my theories.[7]

It is important for Black women, especially, to be represented in the sex-positive movement because understanding the complexities of our sexual experiences and solving for the problematic thinking in our community can be of great benefit to the movement as a whole. Intersectionality is essential here, as sexual liberation is widely regarded as a major key in the complete liberation of women. Women like me—Black women who are comfortable and bold enough to engage in public discourse about sex and sexuality that challenges the status quo—are few and far between. But we *do* exist and our work is important. I have seen more Black women speak openly about their sexuality, share about their sexual experiences (both positive and negative), and declare their rights to experience sex and pleasure on their own terms and not for male consumption. Going forward, my hope is that more attention is paid to the complex, diverse sexual experiences of Black women, and Black people in general, so that we can build a canon of research that helps us reshape and reimagine ourselves as sexually liberated beings no longer restricted by the control others have over our bodies.

CHAPTER 6

# Black Girls Are Magic

*Being a feminist is such a great thing and some people feel like someone
like me can't be as great as that, but then some people are smart but they
don't have no common sense. They think feminism is great and only a
woman that can speak properly, that has a degree, who is a boss, a busi-
nessperson . . . they think only Michelle Obama can be a feminist. But
being a feminist is real simple; it's that a woman can do things the same as
a man. . . . Anything a man can do, I can do. I can finesse, I can hustle.
We have the same freedom. I was top of the charts. I'm a woman and I
did that. I do feel equal to a man.*

—CARDI B, hip-hop artist from the Boogie Down Bronx[1]

**I HAVE BEEN ENCOURAGED TO BELIEVE IN** magic my whole life. From before I could
even speak clearly for myself, I was encouraged to suspend disbelief, to
accept the invisible as tangible, to uphold millennia-old stories as indis-
putable facts, and to accept that the seemingly impossible is absolute truth.
It was the women in my life who pushed me toward this way of thinking.
I was raised to believe that Jesus was Lord—"the Way, the Truth, and
the Light"—and that if I did not believe in this irrefutable idea that Jesus
was the son of God sent to forgive me of my sins with his ultimate blood
sacrifice, I was going to Hell. Hell was a place, I learned, filled with de-
mons, lots of red decor, and a floor that was actually a lake of fire where
sinners burned for their unrepentant transgressions during their time alive
on Earth. Vacation Bible School taught me that when I died, I was going
to have to face Judgment Day, when all of my secrets would be revealed
and all of my sins would be laid bare. So if I did not want to spend eternity

taking a flame bath, I needed to profess that I believed that Jesus was sent from God to be born of a virgin teenager, and also to be crucified so that he could arise on the third day, ascend into heaven, and save us all from eternal damnation. And I needed to be a good girl who did not sneak to watch scrambled porn on my grandmother's television after everyone went to sleep. Seemed easy enough.

I went along with this as it seemed all well, fine, and good until I had a most jarring reality check: snakes cannot talk. Whatever story I'd been taught about a snake, an apple, and a garden no longer made sense because snakes cannot talk. Everything I'd been taught about the people in the Bible and their histories, the plagues and the miracles, the prayers and the curses, essentially became meaningless to me . . . because snakes cannot talk. How could I continue to place all of my hope and faith into upholding the notion that a "God" I could not see, hear, touch, or smell supposedly had my best interests in his mighty plan? And when I considered all of the bad things that had happened to me, even as young as I was, my skepticism grew and I felt my faith wilting and wavering and my spirit began to long for something more meaningful and *real*.

For all of the alleged benevolence God was supposed to bestow upon us faithful servants, Black people seemed to have been skipped over for centuries. Yet don't nobody in this world love them some Jesus like Black people do. We love him so much, we created an entire genre of music and a style of dance just to augment our praise, because that's what King David did to win his favor. This belief is rooted in a religion that isn't really ours, was forced on us during slavery, reinforced White supremacy throughout the nineteenth and twentieth centuries, and, it must be said, helps to maintain White supremacy today.

I began to question this idea of "God," and the spiritual connection that had been forged to this unknown, unseen force began to unravel. I imagined a world in which "God" was less of an omnipotent, albeit overreaching, deity to whom I was to devote my life and more of an internal presence that manifested in my own thoughts and behaviors. I began to feel safer and more comfortable relying on the "me" who I could see in the mirror every day, the person in full control of my next steps, the woman with more power than I was ever allowed to believe I held.

I began to believe in my own magic.

And magic was all around me, though I may not have recognized it as such at the time. The more I studied the history of my people, the more I learned about how diverse our cultural traditions are across the diaspora and just how many of these traditions survived the transatlantic slave trade, slavery in the Americas, and Jim Crow nearly intact or protected and preserved by creative disguises. To believe that our ancestors—who survived such an arduous oceanic journey, followed by centuries of physical and emotional brutality and sociopolitical institutional destruction and disenfranchisement without completely dying off—may have very well been superhuman is not that far-fetched an idea.

I admit that, for a moment, I fell deep into believing the "we were kings and queens" grandiosity. The idea that *all* Black people in the Americas are direct descendants of people of royal blood, wealth, land, and power exemplifies how patchworked are our historical narratives, how piecemeal our cultural traditions are held tightly and closely for lack of any precise, verified connection to our Motherland. While seemingly outlandish to outsiders and dismissed by those well-versed in African tribes, kingdoms, and cultural practices, this thinking is motivated by empowering intentions meant to inspire and galvanize us to reclaim our strength and power. Believing that I was some manner of queen, or princess, at least, made me feel special at a time and in a world when and where feeling special, as a Black girl, was a rebellious experience. Singled out in class by our teachers, picked on because of our hair and skin color, victimized as a result of rumors of our hypersexualization, harassed on the streets by licentious perverts, and invisible in most mainstream media, Black girls aren't supposed to believe they are special or worth acknowledging. So few people truly see us as we are but rather focus on seeing us as they want and need us to exist. Why would we ever believe that we mattered to anyone but ourselves? But as a princess or a queen, people *had* to see me, walking down the street with my kente cloth–wrapped head held high, exuding power and magic, just like my ancestors.

Coming of age during the golden age of hip-hop meant that I was exposed to the teachings of the Five-Percent Nation, also known as the Nation of Gods and Earths, a movement that originated in Harlem in the

1960s and greatly influenced the early practitioners of rap. The teachings heralded Black women as "Earths," the equivalent of "queens," saw Black children as the future who should be nurtured and protected as such, and Black Africans as the original people of the planet Earth.[2] I appreciated the (at least) surface displays of devotion to protecting and loving "Earths," though I questioned the charge for women to keep at least seventy-five percent of their bodies covered.[3] Hip-hop during the early 1990s was filled with Afrocentricity and self-love, immense pride in being Black, and I, too, wore my Africa medallion and called for the United States' divestment from South Africa during apartheid. I even read the controversial *Stolen Legacy* and believed author George James's stories about Greek philosophers "stealing" ancient Kemetic intelligence.[4] What I was looking for was some way of living that would affirm me, as a Black girl turned woman, and make me feel like I wasn't going to have to fight twice as hard, as my mother repeatedly reminded me, because I was both Black and female. I did not want life to be that hard just because I was born into this body at this time.

Discovering the writer Octavia Butler early on opened my eyes to the supernatural possibilities of who and what I could become, even as a Black girl in America. *Parable of the Sower* was my first exposure to her, and the protagonist inspired me and made me believe that Black girls were the future, or would at least be the saviors of mankind. I began to look at the girls and women around me with greater admiration, not only for their ability to endure what had been presented as a curse, but also for their creativity, innovation, and sheer brilliance. I realized that magic was present in the women around me, and I accepted that I inherited a mystical birthright—I was a Black girl! I could make a dollar out of fifteen cents and make a way out of no way because I came from a line of women who had no choice but to do the same to ensure our people's collective survival. And when I was introduced to Ifá, the Yoruba religion centered around the worship of Orishas, or dieties, I knew there were other ways to tap into my own magic, so I embarked on my current journey of learning a prominent spiritual path embraced by my ancestors that remains present in so much of what Black people in the Americas hold sacred.

Black women have endured generations of being treated, by media and community alike, as if we are unworthy of love and respect, are unattractive and undesirable, and we are expected to rise above the negativity and continue to put others before ourselves. We can no longer internalize this hateful, damaging nonsense, and we have to do everything we can to make sure the next generation of little Black girls coming into this world know they are valued, told they are beautiful, encouraged to reach their fullest potential, and embody the "Black Girl Magic" that lives in each of us. Janelle Monáe warned us in her song "Django Jane" that because Whites can't stand our magic, they'll try to deny us the right to claim it. Black Feminism can be a protection and a guide, and as more of us become parents, we have a responsibility to change the narrative, minimize the harm, and shift our culture and communities toward appreciation and respect for Black women and girls everywhere. Bringing our daughters up believing in and never questioning the existence of their own "magic" is restorative and promising, electrifying and declarative, radical and hopeful.

When CaShawn Thompson, a fortysomething mother of two, was growing up in Washington, DC, she knew no other truth to be more consistent and potent than the idea that she and other Black girls like her were magical. It was not a trifle notion of whimsy but rather a truism as commonly understood as fire being hot and humans needing oxygen to breathe. She grew up believing in the fairy tales her parents read to her when she was just a small child, so the lines between reality and fantasy were often blurred for her, and she was perfectly content with that.

In January of 2018, I interviewed Thompson because I wanted to share her story and the origins of #BlackGirlsAreMagic, the hashtag she began to use to highlight Black women's accomplishments and as a rallying call for our empowerment. She was beginning to pick up momentum with being recognized as the creator of the movement, and more people were reaching out to her to include her in conversations, panels, and projects related to "Black Girl Magic." Having known Thompson for many years and having supported the movement from the beginning, I wanted to provide her an opportunity to share her story and clear up any misconceptions about what #BlackGirlsAreMagic is all about. Below are excerpts from our conversation:

**FEMINISTA JONES:** Take me back to the first time you ever thought of the idea that Black girls were magic and what it meant. How did that come to mind?

**CASHAWN THOMPSON:** It wasn't in the four or five years since I have been saying it online; it was probably forty years ago when I was a child, and when I was little, my parents read us fairy tales like a lot of parents do. I was very literal as a little kid, and I thought that Black women were magic. I literally thought because the things I saw happen, what they did, they just had to be magical, just like in the stories I was read as a kid. I never said it out loud because my family already thought I was a little weirdo, but when it came around to present day and something needed to be said about the fantastic nature of Black women, I just said it out loud one day: "Black girls are magic."

**FJ:** And that was it?

**CT:** That was how I had related it to what I saw as a child, and it makes sense today. That's how it came about.

**FJ:** You talk about your family and what they thought about you. What was your situation growing up? What was your early family life like that helped you get to a place where you were just tossing around "Black girls are magic"?

**CT:** Well I was born in DC, where I still live. My family is at least three or four generations deep in DC. I was born to teenage parents; my mother was sixteen, my father was eighteen when I was born. So, of course, I was in a large, tight-knit extended family as well. We lived in my grandma's house with my cousins and my uncle and aunts. My uncles were always around. I was completely enveloped in love as a child. I was favored. I was a favorite child because I was born to the baby of the family. I was really little, and I tended to be kind of sickly in the beginning, so I was one of those favorite children who got almost everything she wanted and had her way and that kind of stuff, like what they would call spoiled.

**FJ:** Did you have siblings?

**CT:** I was the oldest of three. I have a sister and a brother under me. And even then, most of my spoiling came from my grandparents, not my parents. Of course my mother and father thought they gave in way too much to my whims, but you know, that's what happens.

**FJ:** So this was something that you knew from an early age and it just kind of carried you. Tell me about "Pretty Brown Girl," 'cause we cannot talk about Black Girl Magic without talking about Pretty Brown Girl. Tell me how you got into that.

**CT:** "Pretty Brown Girl" was a moniker that I used for myself when I was logging on MySpace, like, ten years ago. It came from my father telling my sister and I that. My parents are very pro-Black, if we are going to call it anything. We were raised to know "Black is beautiful," "Say it loud say it proud," raised in that way, like, completely immersed in Black cultural music, food, literature, everything was always around us. I remember I never had to go away from my people to find myself as a Black person, as a Black girl, as a Black woman. It was, like, literally ingrained in me from birth.

**FJ:** Were your parents involved in any Black organizations or anything like that?

**CT:** I remember them being a part of this organization here in DC called Black Seeds, and we would go to their meetings and their children's workshops and different things like that.

**FJ:** It was like a community organization?

**CT:** Yeah, it was really local from what I understand, and they have a calendar. I think they [her parents] still get it. They had a calendar and they even published some of my mother's poetry. That was way back when.

**FJ:** So they really instilled early on that Black is the truth and you should be happy you're Black? And your dad called you his pretty round girl?

**CT:** Yeah.

**FJ:** When you created the blog on MySpace, what spaces did the blog exist on [after that platform ended]? I know you migrated and you had your own blog. Were there any other platforms that you used for Pretty Brown Girl?

**CT:** After MySpace, I started spending a lot of time on *Very Smart Brothas.*[5] When it first started, in its early, early, earliest days, everybody always thought I had good advice. "Oh you should do an advice column, you should do an advice column," so I had one called "Hey, You Asked." I did that for a little while, and then I decided that I was into nail polish and Black beauty, so I did a nail polish blog called *52 Flavors.* It just started out like that because I wanted to do fifty-two nail polishes in a year, and I did that and various kinds of beauty posts. And then after that, I just wanted to do a lifestyle blog where I put all those things in one spot. I asked a friend of mine, "What would you call a lifestyle blog by me? Something where I talk about life and my experiences and understandings, and also nail polish and makeup and outfits and hair and all that kind of stuff?" She was like "Dirty Pretty Things," and so *Dirty Pretty Things* was a blog I had for a while. It actually won one of those awards. What was that, Black Bloggers Association or something? I cannot even remember.

**FJ:** I think that's how I found you, through *Dirty Pretty Things*, and you know lifestyle blogging became really popular. Do you remember around the year it was that you launched that?

**CT:** It was definitely around 2010. I won something like best new blog that year.

**FJ:** When did you join Twitter?

**CT:** I joined Twitter October 2008, and I did not honestly start using it until the end of that year, beginning of next year, like January of 2009.

**FJ:** And then were you sharing your blog links on Twitter, with people?

**CT:** Definitely. I was sharing my blog links on Twitter at the time, and that's how the word kind of got around. I thought Twitter was the best platform for me because it is for wit and brevity, which people seem to know me for. At least they seemed to at that time, and it worked for me so well. I think organically I just started growing followers because I was able to use the platform so deftly in a time when we still had 140 characters. You remember how it used to be back in the day!

**FJ:** Yes, I remember. Did you use Facebook at all?

**CT:** I used all my platforms. At the time I was using Tumblr pretty heavy. I even made a microblog called *Little Dirty Pretty Things* and I would post just a series of things, like I had, before I met my husband. Before we started dating, I was dating a lot, so I had a series on there about dating, and I had a series on there about conversations on G[oogle] chat between me and my best friend. I used to write book reviews and read a lot of books, so I would write book reviews on there. I had different platforms promoting different things, but they were all related to me and my voice, the things I thought were important.

**FJ:** So take me back to when you first started talking about Black Girls Are Magic or when you first started using the hashtag.

**CT:** I first used Black Girl Magic I want to say June of 2013.

**FJ:** 2013 is coming up in my research too. Someone else had used it before you, but she did not make it popular.

**CT:** The difference was, I was the first person to use it and reference Black girl empowerment. Other times it was used before, it was always something about Black girl's and Black women's hair. I was the first person to use Black Girl Magic or Black Girls Are Magic in the realm of uplifting Black women. Not so much about our aesthetic but just who we are.

**FJ:** Before you started selling the merchandise, how popular was this idea, this hashtag? Did you start seeing other people start to use it?

**CT:** I did see a few people starting to use it, like you and a few other people. It was very like, you know, my homegirls that I talked to on Twitter and that was pretty much it, you and Sydette (@Black Amazon) were using it back then.

**FJ:** What made you want to turn it into merchandise?

**CT:** I think somebody just said listen, it should be on a T-shirt, you know. I had seen other people use Teespring when Teespring first popped off, and I thought, "This is a simple enough way to do this, and maybe I can sell about thirty shirts and my friends will have one; it will be a nice thing to have." But it turned into a lot more than I expected it to. That first [campaign] sold 330 shirts.

**FJ:** How long did it take to sell 330 shirts? Was that in the first month, three months . . . ?

**CT:** That was probably within the first month. Yeah, it did not take long to sell that many shirts.

**FJ:** When people started wearing the shirts and posting the pictures, what was some of the initial feedback?

**CT:** All the feedback I got in the beginning was good. I never got a negative comment about Black Girls Are Magic or Black Girl's Magic until just, was it this year? Maybe last year? Yeah, but all the feedback was positive.

**FJ:** I remember Willow Smith had worn the shirt and put it on Instagram.

**CT:** Yeah that was about two, three years ago.

**FJ:** And so from there what happened? What was the impact of that?

**CT:** To be honest, I'm not sure, 'cause I was pretty confident in its popularity before that, you know, just with us regular girls being into it, so I wasn't like, Oh, this is really gonna pop it off or whatever. I did not really, like, get a serious boost in sales after she did it.

**FJ:** Are there any particular moments that you could look back on that kind of really did give you a boost in sales? Can you think of something that may have happened or somewhere it appeared that you just got like, wow, "I got a boost"?

**CT:** Well, my boosts usually came after some controversy with Black women, like someone had said something negative or nasty about us and the fact that I would go on Twitter and talk about it, you know, talk about how of course this is not true, this is not who we are, this is not how we get down or what have you. And then I would get a boost in sales because of that, after that. So it was always like, somebody would say something bad about us and we want to show them "no," so it is a statement.

**FJ:** What's been your consumer demographic? Has it been mostly women? Have you had a lot of men? If you were to look at the ratio between men and women, what would you say?

**CT:** From what I can tell, it has been like 95 percent women, Black women, and maybe 5 percent Black guys.

**FJ**: Have you had non-Black people, you know like buying and rocking it?

**CT**: Non-Black. Um no. Actually, there were some White women who wanted to wear it, and at the time I made up another T-shirt and I think that it was for White women to wear.

**FJ**: What did it say?

**CT**: "Hint of Spice." And I had a whole story behind that because this guy talked kind of sideways to me and an online friend of mine. Pretty toxic masculinity type of thing and he was just a jerk, let me put it like that. He was being very chauvinistic and patriarchal, and he said in response to what we were saying back to him, I do not even remember the conversation, this is how long ago it was, he said, "Hmm, you females have a hint of spice." So, I put on the T-shirt "A Hint of Spice," and White women bought that shirt. They bought it because I blogged about the conversation, so it gave [the phrase] some background.

**FJ**: But still, overwhelmingly, your base is Black women and Black girls.

**CT**: Yes, yes, absolutely.

**FJ**: All right, so, it grew in popularity, people started buying the merchandise, and you started having other items that you sell. What other items can people buy?

**CT**: Um, mostly sweatshirts, and mugs, and you can buy the mugs from my Facebook page.

**FJ**: Awesome. Okay, let's talk about the backlash. Now, you mentioned you did not start really getting any negative feedback until this year or last year. What kind of negative feedback have you gotten?

**CT**: The only thing that I can remember—well no, it was two things. The first thing, I cannot remember this author's name, she wrote a piece for *Elle* magazine, and she felt like Black Girls Are Magic was just an extension of the strong Black women trope.[6] She felt that it was putting yet another undue burden on us.

**FJ**: I read that shit. All right, I remember exactly what you're talking about. I'll go find that one, all right.

**CT:** That was the first thing. The second thing was I was on Facebook one day, and someone alerted me to this post that this young woman, she was considerably younger than I am, probably in her twenties or maybe early thirties. She had written about how hood girls like her, like regular, shmegular, Black girls from around the way, felt excluded from the Black Girls Are Magic narrative. Like, we're not all Michelle Obama, we do not all, you know, go to brunch and have line sisters and have you know one, two, three, four degrees, and some of us are just living our lives and taking care of our kids and going to our jobs.

**FJ:** I think I remember that too.

**CT:** And that bothered—oh my god to this day it bothered me so much, because when I think about it, I'm a regular, shmegular hood girl who does not have degrees and does not have line sisters and who brunches maybe a couple times a year. And I created it—it was my baby and how dare anyone exclude other Black women [just] because you do not see them as being worthy of it? And I saw other women saying no, they're not a part of it, single mothers this and baby daddies that, and you did not finish school, and why should we celebrate you, and I was like no! No, no, no, that's not what it is. I wrote my one *Medium* post about how nobody is excluded, like no Black woman is excluded from Black Girls Are Magic.[7] I do not care if—What did I say in the piece? I do not care if you're Tracee Ellis Ross and you just won a Golden Globe, or you are Tracy Jenkins, just got employee of the month at CVS. Everybody is included. Trans Black women, Black women who've been incarcerated, Black women who are disabled, everybody's included because it is not all about the glitter and the fame and the popularity. There is not a certain demographic of Black women that deserve to be celebrated by Black Girl Magic.

**FJ:** I think part of why some people felt that way is because when some people would use it, it would be to celebrate accomplishments, right? It would be like a gold medal Olympian and some kind of thing like that, so they started feeling like maybe it was only for celebrating those major accomplishments, but that's not what it was going for. I remember when you pushed back a bit on that. I think this kind of goes into the idea of Black Girl Magic. How it became truncated, you know? Because you went from the concept that "Black girls are magic" is an action—it is an existence, it is a living thing, it is a moving thing which suggests perpetuity, and there are so many things that are tied into the idea of saying that we are magic. So when it is talking about Black Girl Magic as a thing, as a noun, it almost becomes a commodity, and I think there is definitely a difference between that. I'd like your thoughts on how it has shifted, in the larger media and culture . . . , from Black Girls *Are* Magic to Black Girl Magic.

**CT:** Well, I can say specifically that I think it was truncated just for brevity's sake on Twitter because we were confined to those 140 characters, and I think that was like the first thing that made it short, nothing else. Black Girls *Are* Magic was my initial statement, was my initial idea.

**FJ:** And so it has been everywhere. I have seen movies that have talked about it. I watched *Boy Bye*, and one of the characters was talking about "You've got that Black girl magic."[8] I was like ahhh shit. You know, it is funny. I'll see it pop up in these kinds of things or magazines or award shows like *Black Girls Rock!* and other things they talk about Black Girl Magic like—

**CT:** That's a trip also because Beverly Bond [creator and executive producer of *Black Girls Rock!*] and I, our lawyers are in this legal battle over the trademark of Black Girl Magic.

**FJ:** I remember when I first heard that she was trying to trademark it and I remember personally feeling so incredibly disappointed, you know. Just kind of, like, it be your own people.

**CT:** Right. That's been my feeling about it the whole time. Without saying too much, I can say that that whole thing with Beverly Bond and *Essence* also has been completely disappointing. I know for a fact that *Essence* is very aware of [its origin], and the fact that they have tried to monetize and trademark it above and beyond me and before me, you know, it is just disappointing.[9]

**FJ:** "Black Girl Magic" has become the way we talk about Black women. It is the way we talk about Black girls. It is the new way of uplifting Black girls and Black women. Speak to why it is important for us on our own to uplift ourselves, but also to make sure that we are inclusive of all girls. Why does that remain important to you?

**CT:** Well, of course I think it is important for us to lift up ourselves because we live in a society that would rather [we] just plain old rather not. It has as many reasons why, but it just boils down to it would rather us not be celebrated, despite our contributions, despite our power, despite all the things we do, have done and can do in the future. Black girls? Just not important to the world. . . . I say this all the time, "Black women ain't got nobody but each other," you know? So, it is our job to bring each other in and lift each other up. No Black girls should be excluded in that. Absolutely none. All Black women have a story. You have contributions. You have accomplishments. They may pale in comparison to what you see on TV or what you read in magazines online or whatever, but they're yours and they matter. And I do not think that just because there are these people who hold these narrow definitions of womanhood or what's appropriate or what's gonna fly on this day, depending on your mood or what have you, that anyone should be feeling left out. We all should be there lifting each other up.

**FJ:** Right, and I think what Black Girls Are Magic does is it challenges that idea that it does not pale. Like you said, Tracy getting employee of the month at CVS should be as important as Tracee getting a Golden Globe. These things, it is about how we define success and how we define ourselves for ourselves, and I think that that's really the premise of the whole movement, at least my connection to it and my experience with it.

**CT:** That's pretty accurate though. That's definitely it for me.

**FJ:** Do you identify as a feminist or a womanist?

**CT:** Yes, absolutely, absolutely. I did not always, and I tell people this all the time, that I did not come into feminist understandings and womanist understandings until maybe eleven years ago. Before then, because I have a very conservative mother, believe this or not, before then, I thought feminism was a White woman's movement and it did not do much for us, blah blah blah. I remember, specifically, Jamilah Lemieux and another girl, Nikia White, like telling me, "Read this book, read that book. You're going to change your mind because this is who we are and this is what we have done," and sure enough, all I needed to do was like expand my understandings to come into it. So I definitely identify as a feminist and a womanist.

**FJ:** I think that's the story that I'm going to be writing over and over in this book, because I think that is very real. There is something to be said, again, as I'm looking at this academically and historically, I think there is something to be said about Black women's evolution of consciousness as it relates to how we experience our own womanhood and why we may identify with certain things versus other things. But, ultimately, when we affirm and say, "Yes, I am a feminist; I am a womanist," we are staking a claim and our right to identify in that way even if it is a different process for us to come to that. Because of Twitter and social media, those of us who have long histories of being feminists—those of us who have studied feminist theory and women's studies and things like that—we have been able to share our thoughts and ideas and give these recommendations to help other people kind of come into this ideology and have access to it in a way that they may not have, so I'm definitely working on that.

**CT:** That's definitely how I came into it. When I was growing up, it was all about being Black, Black, Black, Black. But it was never about the unique struggles of being a woman and being a Black woman. Then womanhood and girlhood and all those things came secondary to being Black. My mother is still like that. It is hard. But if it had not been for my interactions in online spaces, I do not know how I would have come into it.

**FJ:** Where would you like to see things go [for the future of Black Girl Magic]? Where would you like to see yourself positioned by then?

**CT:** To be honest, I do not know. I'm at a crossroads with it right now. I had a fleeting thought the other day, like, what if I just sell the licensing for it, take a chunk of money, and be done with it. A lot of time I get discouraged because it has been ripped off so many times, and so often by just the weirdest people for the weirdest reasons, and I feel so out of control and unable to do these things. . . . I'm pretty old to be having this crisis.[10]

■  ■  ■

If we are to believe Stevie Wonder's conception of magic, Black women hold the keys to every door throughout the universe. We are as magical as the poet's endless rhyme and the galaxies in time. We fill you up without a bite and quench every thirst. If we are special, though, then why aren't we more careful with ourselves? And why does the world often seem to be proactively engaging in efforts to deny us the right to exist proudly with such glowing essence? The moment Black girls and women believe in our magic is the moment we cease being the reliant workaholic mules, the soothing, nurturing mammies, the all-knowing sage advisers, the stress-releasing punching bags, the stationary props on other people's sets—we believe in our right to say no without being convinced that saying no to others will translate into a lifetime of doors closing in our faces and opportunities fading away.

Hashtags like #BlackGirlsAreMagic or the more popular, abbreviated version, #BlackGirlMagic, serve as a call to action for Black women. They function as a reminder of our power and our unique beauty, internal and external. When Black girls and women make the news, breaking barriers and making history, we highlight their accomplishments with these hashtags. When Black girls and women show up, for ourselves and for others, we want the world to know this is who we are and how we have always been. We do not have to be supernatural or superhuman to be magic—we just need to be. The continuation of our mere existence is magical in itself, and the ways in which we are able to shine and thrive, against all odds, should be honored and celebrated. What started as a hashtag has transformed into a movement that has changed how we speak about Black girls and women, and the world is beginning to *see* us and appreciate us for all of our contributions to forward progress. There is so much that would not exist were it not for us, and sometimes we just need a reminder that we are, indeed, magic.

CHAPTER 7

# Twenty-First-Century Negro Bedwenches

**W**HILE BLACK WOMEN HAVE been highly successful in turning social media sites and applications into personal and professional platforms, their efforts have not been without opposition from detractors and those who challenge your right to exist and freely speak your mind. When you identify as both a Black person and a woman, you should expect to be met with naysayers and antagonists who are wholeheartedly invested in countering whatever messages you might be sharing with others just because you are Black and you are a woman. As your visibility in these spaces increases, so does your vulnerability, and when you primarily identify with two groups that have faced centuries of discrimination and abuse, you become exposed to whatever hate-filled messages people decide to throw your way. One day it could be a White man calling you a monkey, suggesting you should be lynched. Another day it might be a White woman calling your son a "thug," even if he is only six years old. The day after that, it may very well be a Black man calling you an agent of White supremacy simply because you identify as a feminist.

Over the years, I have learned to let most of it go in one ear and out the other, but there are times, I will admit, when these comments really get to me; they strike a chord deep within me and I cannot help but react either publicly or in a venting session with my friends. I have been told that I need to develop a thicker skin, but I counter that by saying it is not that I need to grow stronger and more immune to these attacks—rather, these attacks should not be happening at all. There are people who perpetrate anti-Blackness in their online engagement, citing all kinds of alternative facts and ahistorical "truths" that support their abject hatred of Black people. There are also those who inject misogyny into their interactions, finding as many ways as possible to show the world (or anyone watching) how much they hate women. When you're a Black woman on social media, especially on a platform like Twitter where so many people have access to anything you share at any given moment of the day, you're susceptible to attacks from all sides; these attacks are either racist or sexist or, in the case of misogynoir, both.

When it comes to social media platforms, the onus of responsibility for minimizing online harassment and abuse is put on the victims; most of the messaging teaches you how to block or mute people, how best to avoid "trolls," how to adjust your preferences and privacy settings, and more advice along those lines.[1] Imagine, then, downloading the Twitter application and feeling a sense of urgency to make sure that words like "nigger," "cunt," "bitch," "coon," and "bedwench" are muted, just so you can avoid having to read anything tweeted to you that contains this language. You do not know if the tweets contain an attack, a quotation, or a sarcastic joke, but that's the risk you take to make sure you do not have to see any of it and can avoid the experience of having to deal with the messages that *do* contain hateful attacks. The best thing a Black woman with high visibility can do to preserve her own mental health is to put into place protections that can make her social media experience more enjoyable, productive, and fruitful, so blocking, muting, and filtering act as armor that guards us from unwanted engagement.

I have long been aware of the various slurs and insults hurled from the mouths and fingertips of bigots, so there are some standard terms that I know to avoid. I never imagined having to mute and filter the word "bedwench," though, and it wasn't until the fall of 2013 that I even discovered this term being widely used in serious-minded ways. At first I thought it was a joke, when I read a Black man refer to a Black woman as a "Negro bedwench." Why would a Black man ever refer to a Black woman in such a way, particularly one who claims to be about Black liberation and uplifting Black people? While I did not fully understand it at first, deductive reasoning gave me a general sense of what it could mean, and after doing a bit of research I learned that the term was being used as a derogatory labeling of Black women who these men believed were willingly offering themselves to White men for sexual pleasure. More broadly, these men label Black women they believe are somehow working to uphold White supremacy and are "agents"—spies or plants paid by White individuals and entities like the FBI or CIA—to "destroy the Black community."

"Negro bedwench" stems from the misguided notion that there were enslaved Black women who willingly became their masters' mistresses and enjoyed the so-called "benefits" of being their concubines. Despite everything we know and understand about people in bondage being unable to legitimately consent to much of anything demanded of them by those who owned the rights to their bodies, these men are adamant in their assertions that Black women happily hopped into bed with their masters and strove to be awarded such a position. They have even taken to using the term "bed buck" to describe gay Black men who have sex and/or romantic relationships with White men and who they believe are working against the Black community because of the "rewards" gained by being a bedmate to a White person.

I have studied enough slave narratives to know better. Yet I find myself still utterly appalled at how anyone who claims to be a soldier for Black liberation could use such terminology against their fellow people in the struggle. I have read the words of people born into slavery recounting their own experiences with sexual violence and bearing witness to those types of brutal acts. Preteen girls forced to endure sexual exploitation by the men who owned them, their sons, and their employees. Women whose hearts belonged to men also living in bondage having to mentally disconnect in order to fulfill sexual obligations to their masters, wondering if they'll ever be truly loved and accepted by their chosen mate after enduring physical degradation. I imagine all of the girls and women who felt abandoned by the God their mistresses demanded they pray to, as their masters forced them into sexual service, and I have to wonder what I would have done in those situations. I think it is easy to say "I'd fight back" or "I'd cut his dick off," but would I? How privileged are we to even be able to reflect upon those dark times and imagine the ways we would have resisted a brutality we cannot even fathom? As bell hooks notes, "Since the White male could rape the Black female who did not willingly respond to his demands, passive submission on the part of enslaved Black women cannot be seen as complicity."[2] Yet there are people who assert that our ancestors willingly consented to engage in such behavior, as if they were ever able to say "no." The inability to say "no" renders any consensual intention null and void, yet these simpletons carry on this false notion that our ancestors aspired to be "Negro bedwenches" as a career choice.

W. E. B. Du Bois wrote passionately about the rape of enslaved Black women and the impact on not just women, but the entire enslaved community. In *Dark Water: Voices from Within the Veil*, Du Bois's rage is palpable as he reflects on the inhumane treatment of enslaved Black women:

> I shall forgive the white South much in its final judgment day: I shall forgive its slavery, for slavery is a world-old habit; I shall forgive its fighting for a well-lost cause, and for remembering that struggle with tender tears; I shall forgive its so-called "pride of race," the passion of its hot blood, and even its dear, old, laughable strutting and posing; but one thing I shall never forgive, neither in this world nor the world to come: its wanton and continued and persistent insulting of the black womanhood which it sought and seeks to prostitute to its lust.[3]

He also affirmed:

> The uplift of women is, next to the problem of the color line and the peace movement, our greatest modern cause. When, now, two of these movements—woman and color—combine in one, the combination has deep meaning.[4]

While Du Bois certainly did not have an impeccable track record when it came to engaging women as peers and equals, validating and dignifying them with the respect and honor they deserved as thought leaders, paradigm shapers, and contributors to forward progress, he at least exhibited a healthy awareness of how racism and sexism work in concert to subjugate

Black women. There are times, though, when I read his work and identify his complicity in the very subjugation he rebuked. I wonder if his concern for Black women was primarily rooted in sincere care and concern for us as individual human beings deserving of the same freedom and human rights afforded everyone *or* if his laments and calls for changes were more rooted in a patriarchal compulsion to "protect" Black women, as a display of honorable manhood. That is always the tricky part when we encounter Black men who go on about Black "queens" and "Nubian goddesses," especially—are they adamant about our liberation as long as it doesn't free us from their control? Or are we generally regarded as individuals who exist beyond tangible familial and romantic connections? I mention Du Bois here because he was an early Pan-Africanist scholar who did include early-twentieth-century Black feminist Anna Julia Cooper as part of his international delegation, and their interactions were not always polite and kind. For one, in the same work where he laments the treatment of enslaved Black women by brutal White men, he completely erases Cooper's contribution to this theorizing, referring to her as "one of our women" when he cites her words. Such is the tension between modern Pan-Africanists and Black feminists, enduring a century of philosophical and practical back-and-forth. These men struggle to affirm women as equals but will fight for Black liberation on the whole, intentionally ignoring that sexism exists within our communities, as it does in all, and that Black men are quite capable of oppressing Black women. Their usual response? "What power do Black men have to be able to oppress Black women?" They argue that because Black men have no "power" in greater society (read: wealth, access, and success on par with or greater than White men), they don't have the ability to subjugate Black women. This is complete bullshit, of course, and the mental gymnastics that go into even formulating such nonsense is indicative of ignorance and lack of exposure to historical truth and possibly sunlight.

The "Negro bedwench" caricature is a bit old-school, but the term gained traction when the television series *Scandal*, created by producer Shonda Rhimes and featuring Black American actress Kerry Washington as Olivia Pope, began to rise in popularity. The show centered on a White Republican president who was having an affair with a Black woman known for solving political drama and getting major figures out of trouble or making them pay for their errant ways. Because of the interracial dynamic, *Scandal*'s Black female protagonist was deemed the epitome of the "Negro bedwench" to some viewers, including a subgroup of Black Twitter derisively known as Hotep Twitter (a nickname I gave the group in 2013, using the term "Hotep" in this context to identify Black Twitter users who glorify or skew Pan-Africanism and Afrocentrism in the service of queerphobia and misogynoir). Washington's character was, according to Hotep Twitter—which is composed not only of Black men but also Black women who have internalized the misogynoir rampant among this group—submitting to White male supremacy, and Black women were celebrating it as an accomplishment.[5] Consequently, "Negro bedwench" became a popular insult for women who openly identified as Black feminists because of the notion that Black Feminism is not a "real" concept and exists only to serve White supremacy. It has even been used to describe Black women who wear weaves and makeup, Black women who cosplay, and pretty much any Black woman who does not exist as the "queen" Hotep Twitter believes she should be.[6] It has also been used as a catch-all for any Black woman who has a White male partner, as was the case when Meghan Markle married into the British royal family. Without skipping a beat, the ashy-knuckled dwellers of the Facebook caves emerged to assert that Markle was indeed a "bedwench," despite having nothing to say about her, her career, her feminist activism, or even her name before she was linked to Prince Harry. Since they're authorities on bedwenches, I guess they get to make the rules about the criteria that gets a woman labeled as such.

In 2013, Shafiqah Hudson wrote about and criticized the absurdity of the "Negro bedwench" idea in *Ebony* magazine, noting that most enslaved Black women saw no privilege in being forced to endure sexual assault by their masters, and that most Black women today do not believe they are somehow better than other Black women simply because they date White men. She pointed out that not only were women like Olivia Pope considered bedwenches but also women like Serena Williams, Oprah Winfrey, and Melissa Harris-Perry.[7] It seemed, then, that Hotep Twitter could easily assign this label to any Black woman with success, prestige, wealth, intelligence, and power, and they could minimize her accomplishments simply by suggesting she has only been successful because of her proximity to Whiteness.

The article came out around the same time I had the negative Twitter exchange with a popular Hotep Twitter figure I will call "Talib McAshy." McAshy had tweeted to me, bell hooks, and Jamilah Lemieux together, calling us out for being Black feminists. Hudson witnessed the online exchange and was troubled by the things he wrote to and about us, and decided to write more about him and the Negro bedwench idea.

I cannot recall the tweet specifically, and it has since been deleted, but I remember wondering who he was and why he was coming for me so publicly. Usually, when I have had no interactions with someone, I do not bother to respond to their tweets, but when I clicked his profile, I saw that he had over a hundred thousand followers, so I was intrigued. I did a quick Google search and found out that he was popularly known for writing books about "macking" women and had done the talk show circuit, visiting shows like *Late Night with Conan O'Brien*, to discuss his ideas, which were standard pickup-artist fare. He catered to Black men, primarily, and as I perused the samples of his books, I realized that he was basically teaching men how to manipulate women—his "teachings" were filled with disgusting misogyny and old-school pimp ideas about how to "handle" women.

I laughed. I admit it. I thought McAshy was the most ridiculous person, and when I watched clips of him on television, I could not believe that he sat there with a pimp cane and cup, wearing a flashy suit, teaching White men how best to "mack."[8] That was his claim to fame for years, but I learned that McAshy had reinvented himself, perhaps, as a "conscious" pro-Black activist of sorts. He called himself a filmmaker, having produced a series of documentaries that feature controversial pundits, self-proclaimed Pan-Africanists, a couple of legitimate thought leaders, and a great deal of fallacy.[9] The series made enough of an impact to transition from straight-to-DVD merchandise for barbershop hustlers to being shown in a handful of theaters across the country. With each new film, he gained more traction, likely due to his audience growing and his reach expanding on social media, his pimped-out podcast, and the fierce loyalists who sing his praises everywhere they go.

Though the series has made several intellectual and academic missteps, it has been quite popular among a certain demographic that clings to this so-called knowledge as affirmation. For example, one of the films makes a serious reference to "Willie Lynch," the fictional slave owner created by Dr. Kwabena Ashanti in 1970, and it attempts to legitimize the associated "Willie Lynch Theory," which we also know is false.[10] Yet, this group is fiercely loyal and they defend this reference, moving the goal posts to suggest that though they know Willie Lynch did not exist, the effects of what he was said to have created did and do exist, so it does not matter that the entire theory was made up in the twentieth century during the civil rights era. Facts do not really matter to this group, I learned almost immediately. There is little regard for historical truth, research, data, or anything that can prove their assertions wrong. What I do know is that many of his followers struggle with literacy (as evidenced by their written communication), lack research skills (they often counter well-researched argument with accusations of reliance upon the "White man's research," even when conducted and presented by a Black person), and prefer to hear things that make them feel good about being Black in America rather than things that may present a painful truth.

The grim reality of this compelled me toward empathy. As a social worker whose career has been primarily focused on people who grew up in poverty and who lacked access to the educational resources many of these men could have benefited from, I was more open to accepting that maybe they were just ignorant and not necessarily willfully existing in an alternate reality where facts do not matter and anyone with a YouTube channel can play a significant role in shaping their identities. To this day, there are still some Hotep Twitter devotees I encounter who I believe can be reached and may change their minds and accept new ideas, if only given the chance to access materials that meet them where they are and affirm them at the same time. I have had enough men approach me with gratitude and humility, admitting to having previously subscribed to harmful ideas about women and manhood. This has always been a goal of mine, especially when people my work reaches are those Black men who are written off, who lack access to academia, or who face institutionalized discrimination. Ignorance breeds violence, and the men who have been denied opportunities to exist in the ways society demands they exist to prove their "manhood" are more likely to inflict harm on the women in their lives as a result of their experiences. Women living in poverty are more vulnerable to intimate-partner violence, as studies have repeatedly shown; when men experience economic hardships, the threat of intimate-partner violence increases for women, and men living in perpetual economic stress are more susceptible to violent outbursts against the vulnerable people in their lives.[11] Though many of my peers have completely given up on these men, and I completely and wholeheartedly understand why they have and I respect their choices, there is still part of me that believes a difference can be made. It *must* be made, if only for the sake of our women and children.

However, it was my encounter with McAshy that soured me and even hardened me over the years; I grew less and less willing to educate and explain anything about Black Feminism, because I realized several things: (1) The men weren't really listening to or reading anything I was saying and writing. (2) They specialized in gaslighting, and their pretense of wanting to be educated was a ruse to infuriate me. (3) My tweets were being screenshot and taken out of context to rally trolls and instigate storms of abuse. (4) Many of the accounts weren't real; I suspect McAshy and others have sleeper accounts they use to engage in back-and-forth exchanges to ruffle the feathers of Black feminists (and to boost support for their main accounts). When I decided to publicly respond to McAshy's initial "call-out," for example, his first response to me was a sarcastic comment that my hair wasn't real, and he went on to make comments about my body and my weight before outright denying that he ever reached out to me at all. In fact, he asserted that I began threatening and attacking him out of the blue. I knew then that I was dealing with someone who operated in an entirely different reality than I did and that he—and others like him—would be a problem.

What is "Hotep Twitter," precisely? Simply put, it is a group of people within the Black Twitter community who focus on sharing their so-called Pan-Africanism, much of which is inconsistent with legitimate Pan-Africanist philosophies. They maintain that Africans across the diaspora are supreme, regal, originators of everything, and are all descendants of kings and queens with Egyptian hieroglyphs encoded into their DNA.

Everyone descends from kings and queens, according to Hotep Twitter, so they're often found calling each other by those terms. This does not seem entirely bad, and as I have mentioned before, I once subscribed to a lot of these ways of thinking. Hotep Twitter is, however, rabidly antifeminism, having been convinced that feminism is a conspiracy designed by White women to destroy the Black community. They're often found suggesting that Black women are pawns for White women, acting as agents trying to destroy Black families with our silly notions of equality and gender parity. Hotep Twitter struggles with spelling and can never seem to add the "s" to "feminists," and they're known for believing in wild conspiracies and radical ideas. One young man even offered that women's menstrual cycles are unnatural and only happen because women do not eat healthy enough.[12]

Hotep Twitter is also violently anti-LGBTQ, and their queerphobia and transmisogyny is antithetical to Black liberation. They antagonize organizers like DeRay Mckesson, not because they disagree with his ideas about Black liberation, but because he is gay. They criticized the leadership of the Black Lives Movement, not because they had any significant issues with the movement's platform, but because at least one of the founders of the Black Lives Matter organization identifies as LGBTQ. Once a person is known to identify as queer, their whole life is picked apart and whatever good they do or whatever important ideas they share are subjected to microscopic criticism simply because they exist openly as a nonheterosexual or transgender person.

Black Feminist Twitter and Hotep Twitter have since been at odds, with McAshy and others occasionally sparking controversy by hurling accusations of nefarious actions toward prominent figures in Black Feminist Twitter. In 2014, I launched my anti–street harassment campaign, #YouOKSis, which called on people to pay special attention to the street harassment experiences of women of color. With a rash of assaults and murders happening to Black women, especially, as a result of rejecting men on the street, the issue caught a lot of attention and the hashtag became a popular trending topic. Terrell Starr, working as a freelance reporter for *NewsOne* at the time, wrote an article about Black women's experiences with street harassment and centered the #YouOKSis campaign in the reporting.[13] In his article, he cited Holly Kearl, a White feminist activist who has also been working to end street harassment. Though he only mentioned her in a couple of sentences, Hotep Twitter decided that her inclusion was proof that Black feminists were aligning with White supremacy to criminalize Black men for simply wanting to speak to women on the street. While a completely absurd assumption, considering how we were not interesting in centering anyone but ourselves and our own stories, McAshy managed to convince his followers that I was some ringleader trying to turn Black women against Black men—as an agent working for either the CIA or the FBI (they can never decide which one)—and that I was an enemy of the Black community.

As a result, I endured months of harassment, both online and offline. During an online chat we hosted on July 7, 2014, Hotep Twitter came out in force to try to derail the conversation we were having. They sent thousands of tweets, ironically helping #YouOKSis become a trending topic, and made ridiculous accusations about our intentions, hurled insults about our looks, and tried to convince people that our stories, our lived experiences, were not real. It was hurtful and I could not understand why this man and his minions seemed to be so obsessed with me that they would intentionally set out to harm me and other Black women who were sharing our pain. I had only just learned of him the previous fall, and since that time, he would periodically attack me, disparage me during his podcasts and videos (one video spent twelve minutes declaring me an agent planted to destroy the Black community), make negative comments about articles I'd written about Black women, and incite his followers to harass me by presenting me as Hotep Twitter Enemy Number 1.

My tongue-in-cheek ridiculing of Hotep Twitter slowed down after a professor I respect called out the use of "Hotep Twitter" as an insult. Dr. Greg Carr, associate professor of Africana studies and chair of the Department of Afro-American Studies at Howard University, took to Twitter to share his thoughts about the use of "Hotep Twitter" to criticize this ignorant group of people. He insisted that "Hotep" is a word that means "peace" and is an ancient greeting between people. He has gone on to explain that turning the word into a catch-all insult for a group that is misogynistic, queerphobic, often classist, and ignorant about most things is wrong and harmful to our historical legacy. C. R. Sparrow, in recalling a conversation she had with a coworker who used the word "Hotep" to refer to someone, wrote that she pushed back against the use of the word: "I know what it means on Twitter and social media, but it is actually an ancient Kemetic err Egyptian word that means 'peace.' It means 'peace' or 'of peace,'" said Sparrow.[14] I heard more of this critique from others and I understood where they were coming from—it was, after all, *exactly* why I used the term as I did. I was ridiculing them for overusing the word, completely bastardizing what it represented, and hiding behind it to mask their abhorrent words and behaviors. I own my part in making the idea of "Hotep Twitter" spread as it did, and while I do not regret the original riff I had on #HotepTwitter back in 2013 (because it was really funny and some of my best humor work), I concede that there is a better way to go about confronting the violent misogyny and queerphobia internalized and perpetuated by a group of people who have not been afforded access to the resources, mentors, and educational opportunities that might have set them on a different, more intellectually sound and informed path of consciousness.

Over the years, I and other women I hold in high regard have had to endure the fallout of Hotep Twitter's antifeminist stance. We have learned to write it off, for the most part, but the fact that these people are able to capitalize off antagonizing us is incredibly problematic. For instance, when the conflict surrounding #YouOKSis took place, I realized McAshy was trying to promote his latest documentary installment, so attaching his name to the hashtag put him into the spotlight. I realized that his modus operandi is to use this kind of negative engagement to propel his projects and get his name circulating, and he has learned that Black women are valuable marketing tools on social media. By attacking us, he'll elicit a response that could possibly bring him to new people who might be interested in whatever he has to sell at the time. We ignore it and keep moving forward with our own work, but that does not always work out the way we intend.

In 2016, I became very excited about the release of *The Birth of a Nation*, a movie written and directed by Nate Parker, chronicling the life and legacy of Nat Turner. As someone who has studied Turner and had been itching to see a movie produced about his life, I knew that I wanted to be a part of making sure it got as much exposure as possible, and that Black people everywhere would go see it. Without having seen the movie, I wanted to show my support based on the previews—with films about Black people's experiences with American enslavement being so few and far between, the Black studies scholar in me feels compelled to support *all* of them in some way. I leave room for critique, of course, but I do not believe we can ever have enough "slave movies," and this one seemed to delve even deeper into the grotesque nature of American enslavement, which I believe we have not scratched the surface of uncovering.

A close friend of mine and I decided to work together to develop a marketing plan to promote the movie, #ImWithNat, a play on the popular "I'm With Her" mantra used to support Hillary Clinton in her 2016 presidential campaign. She and I worked to develop a plan that included organizing film premiere buy-outs, panel discussions, and forums on the movie. We were excited for what was to come and happy to provide the pro bono labor needed to make it happen. Another close friend of mine learned of what we were doing and, because she knew Parker personally, decided to connect us with him. We discussed our plan over the phone and he made sure we were connected with Fox Searchlight—they wanted to work with us because our plan was gaining a great deal of attention and traction. Black women's use of hashtags make movements happen, and we were already doing a better job than the people paid by Fox Searchlight to promote the film.

We had some back-and-forth discussions and just as my partner and I were about to make a proposal for compensation from Fox, we learned of allegations of sexual assault against Parker from when he was in college at Penn State. Though others were aware of these accusations prior to this movie, we were not, and when we learned of them, we made the ultimate decision to withdraw our support and not participate in any marketing of the movie. We'd both seen the movie and were incredibly moved by it, and despite some of the historical inaccuracies, we considered it to be powerful and worth larger discussions that were bound to come from the viewings. However, after learning about the allegations and being uncomfortable with how Parker was addressing them in the present, we simply did not feel we could align ourselves with the project at that time.

Somehow, Hotep Twitter decided that the failure of the film was the fault of Black feminists, and they cited me as a ringleader in bringing the movie down.[15] After several years of putting up with their nonsense, I expected some sort of backlash and blame from this segment. After all, they've managed to blame me for so many other things, this would just add to the list. What I was startled by was how adamant they were that we, Black feminist women who were openly and avidly supporting the film, were somehow responsible for the film not being successful. Not Parker's attitude when he appeared in the news or engaged reporters about the incident, not the incident itself, not the film's R rating, no . . . it was definitely Black Feminist Twitter that single-handedly caused the film to do poorly at the box office. While Parker called the film "a blow against White supremacy and racism in this country and abroad," the film did not resonate with early viewers and film critics as anything "worth the efforts of its defenders."[16] Clearly, the issue was not with us or whether or not we supported the movie or rejected it. The film itself had fallen short in the view of audiences and critics, and Parker did not make it any easier by being aloof and occasionally unapologetic about what he was accused of doing when he was an undergraduate at Penn State.

Once again, we found ourselves being called Negro bedwenches, because we opted out of promoting the film and chose to remain silent going forward. We had, as Black feminists, somehow once again betrayed our people, because we did not fall in line with the plan to elevate this movie, and the Black man behind it, to box office and mainstream success. We did not assume automatic allegiance with a problematic Black man, risking our own reputations as women who are antiviolence and anti–sexual assault, to champion a film that was already receiving poor reviews. And this is how Hotep Twitter functions as antagonists of Black Feminist Twitter—they feel they're within their rights to decide which Black women are acceptable manifestations of Black womanhood and which are not. They get to decide who is a "queen" and who is not. And they can make these determinations based on their archaic patriarchal notions of masculinity that they do not realize or refuse to accept are rooted in White supremacy.

What we have learned, through our movement building and our conversations online is that there is a sect of Black men (and women) who do not want to completely get rid of White supremacy; they merely want to paint it black. They envision a world in which they are Black supremacists and can benefit from all of the privileges afforded to White men, just in their Black male bodies. They do not seek gender equality and subscribe to antiquated ideas about gender roles and responsibilities. They want the power they know White men have and they covet White men's wealth (and their women). They aren't at all interested in dismantling capitalism, shattering glass ceilings, or fighting for women's equality—the latter is seen as a direct threat to their already tenuous access to progress and success as men. They have convinced themselves that Black women do not *need* feminism because feminism is only for White women—Black men take care of *their* women well enough that Black women do not have the same problems that White women do. Black Feminism, then, is an affront to their manhood and serves as a public reminder that they *are* responsible for many of the struggles Black women experience and they *are* the cause of most of the direct harm Black women experience, particularly by family members and intimate partners.[17] They hate that Black Feminism has become so visible and widely accessible, because it exposes them and makes them look bad to the world, and they blame us for that.

I spend a lot of time thinking about how we go forward and mend these types of intraracial rifts. Sometimes, I think we will never truly come together as a race of people because even if racism were completely eradicated, sexism would remain. Some other "ism" will serve as a hierarchical measurement of whose lives matter the most. How do we get Black men throughout the diaspora to divest of sexism, acknowledge their male privilege, and commit to unlearning all of the harmful things they've been taught about manhood and masculinity? It is difficult to do when they begin learning these things from birth and often from the women who raise them, who have internalized and long upheld these standards of male supremacy in our communities. These standards are reinforced by media, education, and the society around us and the pressure to adhere to these gender-based guidelines heavily influences how our young people are growing into their identities. Perhaps, through the words we share online and the ways in which we point out acts of misogyny, queerphobia, and internalized anti-Blackness as perpetuated by people who claim to be working on the side of Black liberation, young people will have access to a new way of thinking about these things and be inspired. Because as much as they are exposed to online that is negative and harmful to our progress, they also have access to what we say, so maybe we just need to be more plentiful and louder in our words and actions. I know it works, because I have had so many Black men and younger women come to me and say I helped them understand feminism better and that they have learned more from me than they learned at home or in school. This matters, and it is incredible motivation to keep sharing, because that is how we will strengthen and improve the way the next generation interacts with each other.

# CHAPTER 8

# Black Mamas Matter

**I GREW UP WITH WILD IDEAS** about what my future would look like. I knew I wanted to help people and I knew I wanted to be a writer, but the other details were fuzzy. I knew I did not want to get married or have children, and I'm not exactly sure how I came to that conclusion so early on in life. Maybe being teased or ignored because I was fat pushed me into a space of defending and protecting my heart and spirit from potential pain, so I convinced myself that being married and having children was not only not in my cards, but something I would not even bother wanting.

In 2005, while fully engaged in online communities that celebrated the beauty of full-figured women, I encountered the man who would eventually become my husband. He sent me a cute email on my birthday and we immediately made plans to go out on a date. On April 11, 2005, I thought I'd found the Prince Charming I'd heard so many girls openly dream of. He was taller than my own six feet; he was dark-skinned and bald, just how I liked men. He had a goofy smile, said all of the right things, and his romantic streak swept me off of my feet. We moved fast and furious, and by February of 2006 we were engaged to be married and expecting our first child. I was not only going to be wife; I was going to be responsible for bringing another life into this world, something I simply had not seen happening for myself. Wedding planning went smoothly, but the pregnancy was complicated and high-risk. Due to my obesity and type II diabetes diagnosis, I had to progress through the pregnancy with extra care, and I did—my son was eventually born healthy and beautiful.

I struggled with depression, however, as I was losing my mother to her battle with pancreatic cancer. I would also later find out that my husband had been cheating on me during this time and my marriage was falling apart. I was at the lowest point of my life, and my battle with postpartum depression and grief over losing my mother, who passed away when my son was only six months old, pushed me to my edge.

For the first two years of my son's life, I was unable to connect with him emotionally in the way I would have wanted. My struggles with grief and depression created an emotional barrier between us that I couldn't seem to break through. When my ex-husband and I separated in 2009, I thought life could not get any worse. I was dealing with the worst betrayal I could have imagined, and I faced being another single Black mother in a world that already seems to hate Black mothers, especially single ones. I did not want to be another negative statistic, and looking back, I realized a lot of my anxiety and depression was tied to having internalized the misogynoir reserved for Black mothers. I was terrified, as a nonprofit worker making barely enough money to keep afloat. How was I going to afford rent? Buy food? Take care of my son? My soon-to-be-ex-husband offered financial assistance and I appreciated it, though my soul remained crushed. At the end of 2009, I got a great job making twice what I was making before, and I began to feel better about our future. I knew that, even if my son's father had messed up and decided to back away from his responsibilities, I'd be able to take care of us, and we would be just fine. Still, I had a lot of unlearning to do when it came to the stigma of single Black motherhood, and it was in graduate school that I began to do the work of educating and empowering myself to be the best woman and mother I could be. When everyone around you sees you as being "strong," rarely do they expect you to need help, so they rarely offer it. When you do ask for help, people are often taken aback, unsure of what to do, say, or how to respond to your request.

My ex-husband and I separated and agreed that he would become primary caregiver of our then three-year-old son for a while. Though it was one of the hardest decisions I'd ever made, it was done in the best interest of my son, who did not ask to be born, much less into such a tumultuous time in his mother's life. My mother dying brought a lot of things to the surface for me. I felt like every trauma I'd experienced came back to me, hitting me like a ton of bricks. I wasn't in a good place at all. I knew that in order to be the best person I could be, the best mom I could be, I would need some time to get myself together. I identified the areas in my life that needed improvement—namely my mental health—and took the terrifying, but necessary, steps to heal, grow, and become stronger. When I opened up about this online a while back, there was quite a bit of negative backlash, but mostly positive support. A few people spoke up sharing that they were going through something similar. My ex even wrote a guest post on another blog of mine, sharing his side of things. We were both struck by how many people had a problem with how we'd worked things out for our son. First, it was insulting to him as a father to suggest that he should be allowed less time with our son than I am simply because I'm his mother. Second, it was insulting to me to suggest that I did not love my son or that I was being selfish because I want what's best for him; what we decided was best does not have to fit someone else's ideal, and that should have been understood and accepted. Third, with all of the talk about "fatherlessness" in Black communities, you would think he'd be commended for having such a strong, leading role in our son's upbringing. As many women lamented the absence of their own children's fathers, I admit I was shocked and hurt to read some of them insulting me for making this temporary decision.

I struggled with the dark thoughts convincing me that I was a horrible mother—what mother willingly lets her child's father have more time with him during the week than she had? What kind of neglectful mother sees her child only on weekends? That distorted, backwards thinking was how I'd been raised to regard mothers who aren't primary caregivers. Something had to be *wrong* with a mother who did not provide primary care to her child(ren) because fathers had nothing on a mother's love and nurturing. I'd not yet evolved in my thinking about fathers' roles in child rearing, and as a child raised in the hood among single-mother-led households, the idea of a father having primary custody or providing primary care of a child wasn't an idea to which I could relate or even fully understand.

It was around this time that I began digging deeper into the historical experiences of Black mothers in America, seeking understanding and perhaps answers to the questions I had about my own ability to be a "good" Black mother, according to whichever cultural prescriptions were written for me, even before I was born. I'd heard the "rules" and had received advice, but I thought it important to challenge what I'd been taught, how I'd been raised, and whatever ideas about Black motherhood did not resonate with me. By way of my collegiate studies, I did at least understand that many of the things we understand as guidelines for rearing Black children, particularly as mothers, are deeply rooted in our historical experiences with racism and sexism, and feeling obligated to both protect our children from White society's loathing of them *and* prove that we are, indeed, "good" mothers.

The lives of Black women have been regulated since we were first brought to this new world as servants and slaves. As owned laborers with no access to rights or freedoms, our bodies and production (and those of our children) belonged primarily to White men. Over time, the assumptions about Black womanhood were shaped by our ability to work for and serve White people. Over time, Black women have been denied access to the notion of standard womanhood and femininity; we continue to be seen first as workers, not mothers and wives as White women are. This likely contributes to the lack of empathy afforded Black women who face incarceration and makes for more difficult experiences when others may be granted empathetic leniency. And since, historically, Black women have not been accepted as legitimate mothers or wives, because we had so long been denied claim to our own children and legally prevented from being married, we have not been afforded the same consideration for our humanity as White women.

From colonial times, Black women have had to endure severe physical and psychological abuse that, over time, came to shape not only how they are perceived by others, but how they perceive themselves. They were raped repeatedly as a method of punishment and control, and they had to deal with forced reproduction and accepting that their children did not belong to them.[1] In *Killing the Black Body: Race, Reproduction, and the Meaning of Liberty*, Dorothy Roberts notes that at the same time, Black mothers faced criticism because their actions were deemed negligent as a result of their labor obligations to Whites. Roberts also points out certain issues, such as reproductive rights, were considered "White women's issues." And while White women were expected to form their own families, Black women were regularly denied opportunities to engage in any activity that did not prove to be valuable to Whites, including the development of their own families.[2] Stereotypes about Black women's ability to be good mothers were soon formed and have perpetuated until the present. Angela Davis writes: "The designation of the Black woman as a matriarch is a cruel misnomer. It is a misnomer because it implies stable kinship structures within which the mother exercises decisive authority. It is cruel because it ignores the profound traumas the Black woman must have experienced when she had to surrender her child-bearing to alien and predatory economic interests."[3] She goes on to say that (White) mothers are generally treated delicately, as women are arguably the most physically vulnerable when pregnant, but the Black woman is treated with no more compassion and with no less severity than the Black man.[4] This directly counters the conclusions of *The Negro Family: The Case for National Action* (aka the Moynihan Report), a rather shitty offering by quack sociologist Daniel Patrick Moynihan in 1965.[5] The report suggested that the real problem with Black people was not the legacy of Jim Crow, the systematic disenfranchisement of Blacks across institutions, the general effects of enslavement, or even the rampant racism prevalent at the time of the report, but rather the Black family structure. He argued that the Black family was led by Black mothers and that *that* was the problem, as we supposedly pushed men out of their natural leadership roles, demoted men to secondary decision makers for the family and community, and basically cut their balls off and handed them back to them with a satchel and a few bologna sandwiches before kicking them to the curb. His theorizing exemplified the impact of *Partus sequitur ventrem*, the slave law enacted in the mid-1600s determining that a child's status as slave or free depended on its mother's status at time of birth.[6] Davis further argues that there is no true power experienced by anyone in bondage, be it physical or psychological, so to suggest Black mothers wield *any* power, namely sole power over Black men's ability to achieve and succeed within their communities and greater society, is patently false and designed to create further tensions between two groups of people exerting their energy simply trying to stay alive.

While Davis wrote mainly about enslaved Black women's experiences, the idea of Black women serving economic interests as producers of an exploitable labor force resonates today. We simply need to look at the ways in which America works to ensure reproduction among the most vulnerable and exploitable Black demographic: low-income Black mothers. Begin with the lack of access to preventive sexual education in schools that serve low-income and majority-Black populations, education that, as seen during the presidencies of Bill Clinton and Barack Obama, lowers teen pregnancy and birthrates. Consider the campaigns to vilify and guilt-trip Black women by organizations like the Radiance Foundation, an anti-abortion group that claims to be "pro-life," who use targeted ads on Facebook and other social media platforms to suggest that a Black woman getting an abortion is doing the work of White supremacy. Look into the exponential growth in incarceration rates for younger Black men and women, which Michelle Alexander, writer, professor, and civil rights advocate, identifies as a new form of Jim Crow—a perpetuation of racial oppression barely a step above enslavement—and see how private prisons exploit the labor of inmates to serve many of the largest, most profitable companies and businesses around the world.[7] Finally, think of the war on "entitlements" as fueled by Ronald Reagan–era "welfare queen" rhetoric and reinforced by Clinton-era sanctions on public assistance, and see how this group of Black mothers is systematically trapped in poverty that almost guarantees that one in three of their sons will be imprisoned and the cycle of teen pregnancy will continue.[8] While teen pregnancy is not the end of the world, especially for those who have strong support in and out of the home, it does come with great risks and limitations on economic mobility for the average teen parent, more so for those already living in poverty. These are but a few examples of how Black motherhood often finds itself pathologized as a prescription for struggle and harm when the truth is that it is the racism, sexism, and systemic barriers to socioeconomic progress that have the greatest impact on a Black woman's individual experience with motherhood.

Are Black women allowed to simply be mothers? Are Black women allowed to experience motherhood fully, from conception to rearing, without being subjected to doubt, criticism, or all-out vilification? And are

Black women allowed to become mothers without carrying the burden of perpetually owing someone, somewhere, something? I argue that we are beginning to see a change in the ways in which Black women embark on the journey of motherhood, and the changes are positive and supported by promising discourse and imagery on social media. From blogs that center the experiences of Black mothers, to the pregnant belly pics on Instagram, to the conferences that focus solely on the lives and experiences of Black mothers, we're seeing an increase in positive representation of Black motherhood that directly counters a generation of vilification. Whereas the Moynihan Report burned into people's minds the idea of a dangerous Black matriarch who is primarily responsible for the destruction of the Black family by way of emasculating the Black man, alienating him from his rightful role as leader and decision maker, many Black mothers of today are thriving in loving intimate relationships, being supported by close-knit families, and are the driving forces behind the positive growth of their communities. And they're doing all this while raising Black children who are loved, valued, and come into earlier understanding of their importance to their world and the strength of their own humanity.

Online communities provide safe spaces for Black mothers and have been instrumental in creating support networks for minority women, who often feel left out of mainstream discourses on motherhood. Mainstream websites have long featured content and advertising catering to pregnant women and mothers, though primarily geared to White women and families, and the participants could not always relate to the things Black women share or answer the questions Black women had about their pregnancies and their first years as new mothers. With every topic, from managing the work-life balance discussions to breastfeeding, Black mothers have struggled to fit into many of the major motherhood communities and discussions online. So, as we often do, we created our own.

In the early 2000s Black women were creating our own chat rooms and message boards on sites like Babycenter.com or iVillage.com called "Black Families" or "African American Mommies" to create space to discuss parenting with cultural nuances others might not appreciate or understand. It was in these spaces we could ask questions about taking care of our babies' hair without getting answers like "Ooooh use Johnson &

Johnson No More Tears!" or "Why would you put olive oil on a baby's scalp?!" We could have a nuanced, often heated discussions about spanking and how Black mothers struggle with being ridiculed or accused of trying to parent like White mothers for *not* spanking our children. Despite being accused of being separatist or even racist, in some instances, because we gravitated toward our special interest communities, we continued to find our ways to each other and these spaces that welcomed and connected Black women from all over the world.

Breastfeeding, for example, has been a controversial topic for mothers of all races, but for Black women, it has been a sensitive discussion, given the historical implications of breastfeeding. For centuries, Black women were forcefully disconnected from the experience, having to instead provide their breast milk to the children of people who owned them and later to the children of the people for whom they worked in domestic roles. Not only were they disconnected from their families and denied the opportunities to prioritize the nourishment and health of their own children, Black women were often kept out of engaging in empowering activities that would allow them to advocate for themselves as women, such as the suffrage movement, because they were relegated to serving as wet nurses for White women who *were* marching in streets and attending important organizational meetings. This disconnect led to the point of disgust and resentment for some Black women and the tradition has not always been encouraged intergenerationally. A 2010 study found that only 54 percent of Black mothers breastfed, compared to 74 percent of White women and 80 percent of Latina women.[9] A 2011 study showed that one explanation for the disparities is connected to racial disparities in access to the vital healthcare that supports new mothers' efforts to breastfeed.[10] In neighborhoods with a Black population of at least 12 percent, Black mothers and newborns spend less time in the hospital room together, Black babies are given formula along with breast milk more often, and receive less assistance with initiating breastfeeding.[11]

I recall that when I birthed my own son, I was not visited by a lactation specialist until a few hours before I was discharged and I'd been in the hospital for three days after my caesarean delivery. I struggled with milk production because I had been living with type 2 diabetes prior to becoming pregnant and was informed that it could cause a delay in production. I accepted this information as truth until a Black nurse visited me on my last day and asked if I'd been given a pump or offered help to get my new baby boy latched onto my breast. When I told her I had not, she immediately left the room and returned shortly with a pump and in a few minutes, she had breast milk coming out. By then, however, my son had been fed formula at each feeding and he struggled with latching on. I eventually gave up because my efforts to feed him weren't working and my anxiety was at an all-time high. He ended up needing a special formula because he had early gastrointestinal issues, and it cost twenty-six dollars a can. I do not regret formula-feeding my son, but I do sometimes wonder if I'd received the assistance I needed, would he have been healthier and could we have saved a ton of money.

Between our historical trauma, current social norms, disparate access to healthcare, and interfering health issues, twice as prevalent among Black people as White, the breastfeeding experience can be difficult to embark on and navigate, and it makes sense why more Black mothers opt to formula feed their babies.[12] On these race-specific message boards, new moms could ask each other about the best formula for a colicky baby without having a barrage of White mothers berate them about not breastfeeding instead. Today, there are communities like "Black Women Do Breastfeed," which began on Facebook and grew to have their own full websites, and mothers posting pictures of themselves breastfeeding on Instagram or Facebook that encourage others to embrace the practice.[13] When Karlesha Thurman, twenty-two, posted a picture of herself breastfeeding her baby during her college graduation ceremony in 2014, it went viral, stirring controversy and important conversations. It was a bold move, both to do it and share it online, but she inspired so many others to follow suit and show their photos. I recall some of the discussions being about how we do not often see pregnant or breastfeeding Black women in major parenting or motherhood advertisements and magazines, which has long been a form of erasure of the Black motherhood experience.

Celebrities like Beyoncé Knowles-Carter and Serena Williams have also been influential in changing the image of Black motherhood, as they have given their fans a peek into their pregnancies and lives as mothers.

Both Knowles-Carter and Williams shared photographs of their pregnancies and video snippets of their journeys, while remaining protective of their privacy, as many celebrities prefer to do. Each woman embarked on motherhood in her thirties and at the height of their careers, showing that not only is it possible to "have it all," but that having it all also means doing things when one chooses and when it makes the most sense for both their professional and private lives. Their journeys have not been without criticism and struggle, though, and there's something to be said about how even wealth and success cannot shield a Black mother from being criticized and receiving backlash for various aspects of their journeys.

Like most mothers, Williams worried about whether or not she'd be good at it and even entertained the idea of giving up tennis to be a full-time family woman.[14] Having dreamed of being a mother since childhood, she was very careful and protective of her body during the pregnancy. When it was time to deliver, however, she had major complications that resulted in an emergency C-section, and after delivery, she had even more complications related to blood clots in her lungs. Having experienced a near-death experience with pulmonary embolism in 2011, she was concerned when she had trouble breathing, so she alerted a nurse who dismissed her concerns and suggested Williams was "confused" by the pain medications.[15] Williams pushed the issue and found out that she was not only right, but that she needed emergency procedures that likely saved her life, but meant spending the first six weeks of her daughter's life in the hospital.[16] Her experience is not unlike other Black women's experiences with labor and delivery, as maternal death rates among Black women are the highest of any demographic in the country with Black women being 60 percent more likely to develop life-threatening conditions like high blood pressure and preeclampsia.[17] Between 1987 and 2013, pregnancy-related mortality rates rose from 7.1 women per 100,000 births to 17.3 women, and this climb is driven by the rise in maternal death among Black women, who are now three to four times more likely to die from pregnancy-related complications than White women.[18]

Since the 1850s, when the United States began tracking infant mortality rates, Black babies were 1.6 times more likely to die than White babies, and even with improvement to medical care and general hygiene

practices, Black babies and mothers continue to die during or as a result
of childbirth due to racial disparities in maternal healthcare. Today, Black
babies are more than twice as likely to die than White babies, despite
the overall death rate declining over the last century or so. Black women
are less likely to receive adequate maternal healthcare for various reasons,
with income and access to quality, affordable healthcare being the most
pressing issues. But these disparities aren't limited to lower classes of Black
women; Black women with college degrees are still more likely to die as
a result of pregnancy or childbirth than White women who did not graduate high school.[19] What this suggests is that Black women are vulnerable
due to perceptions of healthcare providers, who have been proven to treat
Black people *and* women differently. Women are less likely to receive pain
medication than men, and are instead given sedatives to calm them down,
as healthcare providers disregard women's complaints of pain as being
emotion-driven hypochondria.[20] Women are also seven times more likely
to be misdiagnosed for heart-related diseases and complications, which has
even more significant implications for Black women who have higher rates
of heart disease.[21] And one study on abuse of prescription opioids found
that Black patients are half as likely to be prescribed pain medication than
White patients.[22] When we consider all of this information and apply it
to Black mothers, especially, it is clear that Black mothers face incredible
odds just to give birth to healthy children, survive childbirth, and have
their children survive past their first birthdays and this is all true in the
twenty-first century when we have access to all of the most advanced
medical technology available to anyone.

Williams sharing her story publicly came at a time when there was more
attention being paid to the terrifying trends in Black maternal healthcare,
and her celebrity amplified the issue and forced the public and media to take
notice that Black women are and have been struggling to bring forth life for
generations. And while many of us have grown up with little understanding of the risks Black women take when they embark on motherhood, as
we have been surrounded by loving and nurturing Big Mamas, Ma'dears,
Nanas, Auntie Pams, and Godmommy Keishas, it is great to see Black
mothers getting more attention and support in efforts to close the healthcare
discrimination gap. And the support systems created and sustained online

play a key role in bringing mothers together to share their experiences and collectively advocate on their own behalf. It begins with changing the narratives around Black motherhood and it continues with creating, building, and strengthening the communities and networks that specifically cater to issues affecting Black mothers in the twenty-first century.

Anthonia Akitunde is a Black female journalist and creator of Mater Mea, a "website that tells the stories of women at the intersection of motherhood and career [that] offers a more realistic depiction of Black women in the many spaces they occupy: as mothers, daughters, employees and employers, lovers, and friends."[23] Launched in 2012, Mater Mea has grown into a hub for all things related to Black women's experiences as mothers, and the high-quality content, including well-researched educational material and intimate profiles of Black mothers from all walks of life, is one of the best sources of information for and about Black mothers. I encountered Akitunde several years ago and was impressed by the work she was doing, so when she asked me to participate in a special project she was doing about Black mothers challenging the perceptions of their Black children, I was excited and honored that she wanted my son and me to share our journey. When Tamir Rice was shot and killed by a Cleveland police officer in 2014 and I interviewed his mother, Samaria, for *Ebony*, I began to feel even more protective of my son, who bears a striking resemblance to Rice. This project allowed me to be proactive in contributing to a narrative that could change the world's negative perceptions of our children. Akitunde's video series was well-received and covered by many outlets, including *Essence* and *Huffington Post*, and it provided a transformative opportunity for viewers to gain insight into what it means to be a Black mother in a time marred by a seeming increase in acts of fatal police brutality and officer-involved shootings of Black Americans. In our interview, I shared that my goal is to raise my son in the feminist tradition and encourage his social, emotional, and cultural learning with regard to his race and place in this world. When I decided to write about key figures in shaping a new narrative of Black motherhood, Akitunde and Mater Mea were the first to come to mind.

Akitunde grew up in a home where feminism was practiced, but not specifically named or discussed—women's empowerment and equity was simply the way of life. Her mother encouraged her in ways that we now understand are feminist in practice, but her primary connection to feminism was through perceptions of White women's interpretation and exhibition of feminist praxis. As a journalist, she was very much interested in the conversations about motherhood and career that were often centering White women. Though not a mother herself, she had intentions of becoming one and wanted to know what it meant to be a Black working mother. Mater Mea was created at the height of the "Lean In" discourse encouraging women to become more aggressive in asserting their positions in the workplace and finding the elusive work-life balance.[24] She noticed that while there were many Black women rising in prominence in various sectors like politics and fashion, rarely did they discuss being mothers as part of their brand. She wanted to have more conversations about work-life balance that focused on Black women and Mater Mea was created because, as a journalist, she wanted to create high-quality content for Black women and mothers.

I spoke with Akitunde about Mater Mea for this book and she shared some of the ups and downs of facilitating these conversations and maintaining this space.[25] After launching the site, she began receiving inquiries by popular (mostly White) publications seeking input on her stories, but it did not always feel genuine. Were they truly interested in diversity or were they simply sourcing her to fill a quota? That tension prompted her to invest more of her time and resources into cultivating the site and turning it into a communal space that reflected the diverse experiences of Black mothers while encouraging discourse among subscribers and visitors and providing support as needed. "Knowing you can go to Mater Mea to ask for help and get answers and support you need to help you get to where you need to be" is one of the greatest accomplishments Akitunde attributes to Mater Mea, and she hopes to see this supportive community grow and continue to uplift Black mothers from around the globe by bringing them that much closer through this digital platform.

"When I started the site there wasn't as much positive imagery around Black motherhood. Now there are a lot more images with an aspirational quality. There is a disconnect between the aspirational motherhood and the lived experience," she shared, and immediately Knowles-Carter and

Williams came to mind. While each of these women presents imagery that makes motherhood seem like the most glamorous of endeavors, the reality can be much more mundane, honestly. Akitunde noted that, in this social media-driven era, a lot of Black mothers feel they need to "slay," so they are more likely to present images and stories that perpetuate that notion. Influencer marketing has more to do with the expansion of seeing imagery around Black motherhood and there are collective Instagram accounts that show Black motherhood and curate imagery that's positive for Black mothers. She also notes that while there are some empowering aspects of the surge in Black mama imagery, there are some blogs and platforms that fetishize motherhood and Black children and focus on a specific aesthetic (biracial, lighter-skinned children). There appears to be, however, a new emphasis on reclaiming motherhood as Black women's joy and not Black women's burden, and the positive changes far outweigh the negative pushback. Akitunde wants to see Mater Mea grow and provide more opportunities for an in-person community, which would shift from the one-sided experience of reading conversations written by her to making herself more accessible for face-to-face interactions with mothers. "Online communities were so important when the site first launched, but now people want that same support in real time, face-to-face."

One woman who has been able to take this community offline is Tanya Hayles, a Black mother living in Toronto, Canada. Hayles created Black Moms Connection (BMC), a digital space that began with twenty mothers and now boasts over ten thousand members worldwide. According to the website BlackMomsConnection.com, the community's mission is to provide "a safe and encouraging environment for Black mothers to connect with shared cultural experiences."[26] It began as a Facebook group in 2015 and became an incorporated nonprofit in 2016. Hayles, an event planner and writer who has contributed to *Blavity*, *Teen Vogue*, and *Today's Parent*, set out to combine her various skills to bring together Black women from around the world to network and engage in discourse about what it means to be a Black mother in today's world. She launched the site because she struggled to find answers to questions she had about child rearing that were race-specific and because she found that she needed support and wanted to cultivate a network of Black moms and children who could come together and have play dates and meet-ups. When she could not find what she needed on more mainstream parenting sites, she did what Black women so often do: she created a space herself.

The first network of its kind in Toronto, BMC gained traction because there was no other community like it in Canada. Many Black moms around the world find they have to rely on America-centered websites to create community, and Hayles's experience was no different. At first, she limited it to Canadian mothers, but as the popularity grew, she opened it up to moms around the world. Hayles found that when it came to marketing campaigns, groups, conferences, and other events that geared toward all things parenting, Black mothers aren't usually included or represented. When she conceived of the Black Moms Connection Conference, she wanted to replicate the vibe of a beauty salon, where Black women could come and keep it real with each other without the influence or interference of outsiders. Some of the past topics have included financial literacy, sex and sexuality, and self-care, which are universal to all mothers. But other topics, like navigating the educational system while Black and dealing with racial microaggressions in the workplaces are not. She and her team choose the panels based on the most popular topics in the Facebook group, which has well over ten thousand members. They try to include as many topics as possible, but with the conference only being one day, it is hard to pack everything in. Still, Hayles and her team try to cover an array of topics that speak directly to what's current and in-demand in the group.

Hayles notes that the BMC conference speakers are all Black women/ women of color, which is especially important as Black women are not usually sought out for our opinions and expertise about parenting. By centering women of color, BMC avoids inviting energy and contributions that Hayles is sure would change the dynamic and energy of the space. The inaugural conference drew over a hundred women and several dynamic speakers and panelists. I was invited to speak and was all set to participate on the Love & Sex panel, but severe weather conditions caused my flight to be canceled at the last minute. I was disappointed because I knew Hayles was making history by hosting the first-ever conference for, by, and featuring Black women in Canada, and I wanted to show my support and connect with more Black women from another country. Having connected with women in Johannesburg, Paris, London, and other international cities, I was eager to add Toronto (and the women there) to my ever-expanding global network of Black women. Hayles received a number of honors and recognition for her work, and she plans to host the conference annually and bring more and more Black mothers together.

Creating and maintaining an online space for Black mothers is not without its challenges, as one might expect. Hayles says that the most negativity comes from White mothers of biracial children who believe they should have access to the space and fail to consider the historical context of their roles as White mothers to children the world sees as Black. Hayles finds their asking Black women they do not know to educate them on how to raise a half-Black child is presumptuous, entitled, and insulting. There is almost a demanding and resentful energy hurled toward BMC when the Black mothers do not feel inclined to engage the White mothers, and whenever BMC garners mainstream media attention, a new wave of attacks and insults comes its way.

Hayles has learned a lot about feminism through social media and identifies as a womanist, and it is through this lens that she is able to process these attacks and compartmentalize them as falling right in line with historical attacks on Black motherhood, which has not been limited to the United States. It is the erasure of Black women from mainstream feminism that compels her to identify as "womanist," and it is the erasure of Black mothers from modern motherhood discourse, marketing, and representation that motivates her to remain forward-thinking about BMC. In the future, she hopes that BMC grows as an organization, with a full board and staff that expands to several chapters across North America, and she hopes to operate a child-care center in Toronto. Hayles believes that the spaces that have been traditionally closed to us, from podcasts to blogs, are now open because of social media and internet access, and Black moms are shaking tables and making their voices heard.

As Black women find themselves feeling empowered to proclaim the joys and struggles of their motherhood experiences boldly, owning their truths about the great moments and the truly awful parts, they are taking to social media and other digital platforms to share their stories and create new narratives of Black motherhood in the twenty-first century. Less than two hundred years ago, enslaved Black women had no claim to their own children and wrestled with their inability to protect their children from harm and sufficiently nourish and nurture those children they were able to keep close. And within the last hundred years, Black mothers have been vulnerable to the racist whims of White liberal social workers who arbitrarily make decisions about Black mothers' fitness. Too often, the state separates Black mothers from their children under the guise of "protective services." In states like New Jersey, for example, where Black children are 14 percent of the minor population but make up 41 percent of those in foster care, Black children are three times more likely to be remanded to foster care despite evidence showing Black mothers are no more likely to engage in behaviors that endanger the welfare of their children than White women.[27] What we continue to see is the systematic separation of Black children from their mothers, which has long-term detrimental effects on the children, many of whom experience developmental challenges at rates disproportionate to that of White children.[28] Because of implicit bias in care provision and service delivery, Black mothers and their children are highly vulnerable when they engage doctors, nurses, social workers, and the like; the perceptions and stereotypes about their racial attributes pose serious challenges to their ability to be the best mothers they can be.

Black mothers have the right to experience healthy pregnancies, have safe deliveries, be protected before and after childbirth, have smooth and fair foster and adoption processes. They have the right to adequate paid time off and access to affordable and safe childcare options, and to know that their children's health and well-being are not jeopardized by the pervasive discrimination that follows from the assumption that Black women and their children do not need the same level of care as White women and their children, which leads to negligence at various stages of their lives. I envision a world in which Black moms and Black children who go missing receive the same attention as White mothers and children who go missing—the world stops spinning and every news channel has nonstop twenty-four-hour coverage that includes interviews with everyone who ever saw the missing woman or child even once. I imagine a world in which Black mothers do not have to choose between working to keep roofs over their children's heads and being satisfactorily present in their children's lives as they grow and develop. I hope to see a world in which Black mothers, and *all* mothers, be they teenagers, trans women, adopting mothers-to-be, married, or disabled are afforded the same access to healthcare, education, and growth opportunities. Mostly, I want to live in a world in which people no longer disregard Black mothers' laments and outcries for support based on a centuries-old assumption that Black mothers not only can "do it all," they *must* do it all, for themselves and for everyone else.

CHAPTER 9

# "I've Always Been Good to You People!"

**I**N THE FILM VERSION of Alice Walker's groundbreaking novel *The Color Purple*, director Steven Spielberg depicts a scene between the character of Miss Sofia, a heavyset, bold, brown-skinned Black woman, and the mayor's White wife, Miss Millie. The confrontation between the two women is sparked by Miss Millie observing Miss Sofia tending to her children, which prompts the former to ask the latter to come work for her as her maid. Miss Sofia, taken aback by the brazenness of the ask, strongly rejects the offer, much to the dismay of Miss Millie. An argument ensues, Miss Sofia is assaulted, and she is ultimately arrested for the crime of telling a White woman no. After spending several years in jail, Miss Sofia is released and ends up working for Miss Millie anyway, elongating her servitude.

Later in the film, after decades have passed, Miss Millie attempts to bestow benevolence upon Miss Sofia by allowing her to spend one full day with her family. Having relied on Miss Sofia for everything, Miss Millie finds herself unable to drive herself home after dropping Sofia off at her family's home. As some of Miss Sofia's male family members try to help her, Miss Millie becomes frustrated and fearful, assuming they mean to attack her. She yells to the crowd of Black onlookers, "I've always been good to you people!" admonishing them for somehow betraying her warped sense of kindness.

Unable to overcome her irrational fear of Black men, she denies Miss Sofia her promised family time by demanding she drive her back home, despite offers from others to provide escort. Defeated, Miss Sofia says goodbye to the family she has not seen in years and dutifully obliges Miss Millie.

This scene has long resonated with me as signifying the ways in which the fragility of White damselhood harms Black women. When Dorothy Roberts wrote, in *Killing the Black Body*, about the Black woman's experience in America from colonial times to the present, she paid close attention to the historical objectification of the Black body; the physical, verbal, and emotional abuses heaped upon Black women; and the exploitation of their labor, primarily for the benefit of White women and their families. Black women's bodies were envied, their femininity denied, and they were made to endure the pain of being forced to prioritize the needs of White women's children over their own (and be blamed for neglecting their own children and later pegged as "bad mothers"). Because Black womanhood has long been measured against a standard for womanhood that is aligned with Whiteness, Black women have been destined to fall short— if "woman" equals "White," not being White means not being *real* women. Being remanded into the service of White women only reinforced that inequality and established a power dynamic in which White women could lay claim to being the gatekeepers of Black women's access to womanhood; for too long, White gatekeepers have rigorously fought to ensure they would never be unseated, particularly by Black women, as the standard with regard to women's beauty, allure, grace, and class.

Black women have been reluctant to align themselves with modern feminist movements because they often do not feel as though their unique needs and concerns are addressed by mainstream White Feminism. But feminism is inherently antiracist, so any reference to a racist White feminist is a misnomer and antithetical to feminism as a theoretical framework. There are experiences that happen to all women for which there are ample advocates and vocal supporters: domestic violence/sexual assault, equal pay, and reproductive justice are three of the key issues that modern feminists focus their attention and efforts on when working to improve the lives of all women. For the most part, modern feminists acknowledge that there are racial disparities in each of these issues, and consideration is given to how the experiences of women of color often pad the numbers used to represent oppression and victimization. Less consideration is given to how Black women have been forced to navigate racism in the women's liberation movement and sexism in the Black liberation movement. In 1925, Amy Garvey, wife of famed Pan-Africanist Marcus Garvey, wrote:

> White women have greater opportunities to display their ability because of the standing of both races, and due to the fact that black men are less appreciative of their women than white men. The former will more readily sing the praises of white women than their own; yet who is more deserving of admiration than the black woman, she who has borne the rigors of slavery, the deprivations consequent on a pauperized race, and the indignities heaped upon a weak and defenseless people?[1]

But let's get back to White Feminism.[2]

If I could make a T-shirt with the words I AM NOT YOUR FEMINIST HERO, I would hand it out to White women like Rose McGowan, Lena Dunham, Tina Fey, Amy Schumer, and everyone behind that godawful 2015 film *Suffragette*, who, for all their good intentions, feminist claims, and rabble-rousing seem unable to *not* say and do ignorant shit. Their privilege as White people affords them the freedom of not having to be made constantly aware that their race can get them killed if they look at a police officer the wrong way. Their privilege as White people often gets in the way of their ability to be truly intersectional in their feminist praxis, because clinging to their Whiteness, if it means lessening their suffering, is just too tempting to pass up. Their privilege as wealthy White people disconnects them from the everyday struggles of millions of American citizens. Even when they are poor, and often vote against their own best interests, being White still affords them access to opportunities to improve their condition that others don't have. And their privilege as White women means the world falls at their feet, begs to wipe their asses after a White Castle Crave Case, and falls off its axis if one of their dogs goes missing. They have no real reason to think outside of themselves, so I am not sure why anyone continues to expect them to . . . #SolidarityIsForWhiteWomen.

When the #MeToo movement reemerged in the wake of a storm of sexual harassment allegations being levied against powerful men in

Hollywood and the music industry, several famous women shared stories of the abuses they'd endured. Rose McGowan, the actress and author of the memoir *Brave*, which includes a recounting of her harrowing experience with film producer Harvey Weinstein, has been especially outspoken in her suggestion that many people were well aware of Weinstein's abusive behavior toward women. Many people had heard the stories but did nothing to support the women he violated or stop him from preying on others.[3] McGowan has described Weinstein as an "international rapist" and "sociopathic predator," criticizing Hollywood's handling of the matter of ninety-plus women accusing Weinstein of sexual violations.[4] She garnered a great deal of support, particularly after it appeared that Twitter administrators had limited her account's visibility and her access to it. Make no mistake, McGowan has been a force in pushing the issue forward, and reading what happened to her makes me sick both for her and for every woman who suffered at Weinstein's hands.

But then she went and tried to make a connection between women's experiences and Black people's experiences. In a response to an October 2017 tweet by Chris Gardner, senior staff writer for the *Hollywood Reporter*, who was pointing out that comedian James Corden was making jokes about Weinstein at a Los Angeles gala,[5] McGowan responded, "THIS IS RICH FAMOUS HOLLYWOOD WHITE MALE PRIVILEGE IN ACTION. REPLACE THE WORD 'WOMEN' w/ the 'N' word, how does it feel?"[6]

Yes, she went there. She went Full White Woman at a time when going Partial White Woman would have sufficed.

As an open supporter of McGowan, I was disappointed but not surprised. She is not the first person to suggest an equivalency between womanhood and Blackness. White women in feminism struggle to unlearn and divest of their privilege, and intersectional approaches aren't exactly organic practice for them. I decided she no longer needed my public support, and maybe I will catch hell for this, but there was no way I could continue to lend my support to someone who seems oblivious to the fact that there are people who exist who are both women *and* Black. Unless you are a Black woman expounding on the intersection of race and gender, I admit I am not much interested in hearing anything you have to say on the matter.[7] Do I empathize with McGowan? Of course I do, especially having endured my own sexual trauma; I would not wish what she went through on anyone, and I hope she receives the justice she deserves. But you can be both a victim *and* an oppressor, and that is something more people need to understand, particularly when it comes to matters related to race or gender. McGowan offered a one-off apology for the tweet, but the sting remained for many of us, and it forced us to consider what our roles and responsibilities would be in the #MeToo movement. Black women have had to navigate rather murky waters to find solidarity and connection with the privileged women, mostly White, who have been the primary focus of sexual-abuse campaigns. It should not have to be this way. Women of all races and classes should be able to come together and fight against the true enemy (hello patriarchy!), but we continue to struggle with finding common ground because of the privileges afforded to some of us and denied others.

That leads me to Lena Dunham, who is a fucking mess and not worth another sentence. So that's that.

Creator of the "HeForShe" campaign, Emma Watson has had a very public (and fascinating) evolution as a feminist. Watson is best known for her role as Hermione Granger in the film versions of J. K. Rowling's popular Harry Potter books, and she has since appeared in a number of projects, including the live-action adaptation of the Disney film *Beauty and the Beast*. The HeForShe movement, with a United Nations–backed platform and a mission, upholds gender equality as a global standard and calls on advocates around the world to "stand together to create a bold visible force for gender equality."[8] I always thought, based on the name, that it was about men stepping up and taking on more of the responsibility of fighting for gender equality, but the three primary leadership roles are held by women and the messaging is more about "everyone" and "all of us." Their hearts and intentions seem to be in the right places, and though I cannot personally speak to the impact of the campaign, I can at least say I have heard of them.

Watson faced criticism for her feminist praxis and, after being called a White Feminist™, she defended herself by saying that she was not exclusionary of Black women, because two Black women have been her bosses. Yes, she did the whole "I'm not racist, I have a Black person living two towns over from me" thing and Twitter reacted. She was called a "White Feminist" because, like so many other White feminist women, she approaches feminism with a #YesAllWomen lens that women of color have repeatedly condemned as being ignorant of the nuances of their experiences. And while White women rely heavily on statistics that exist primarily because of the experiences of women of color (see: wage gap), they often neglect to acknowledge how their privileges can afford them opportunity and resources to advocate for themselves in ways that other women do not have. So yes, Watson was grouped in and labeled a "White Feminist" because she perpetuated the same erasure that has been harmful to women of color since the inception of the late-nineteenth-century women's liberation movement.

What makes Watson different is that she has since been public about acknowledging her privilege and "blind spots" when it comes to the lack of intersectionality in her feminist praxis.[9] She admitted to feeling offended by the criticism at first, but eventually opened herself up to receive and reflect on it. She wrote, in a letter to her book club:

It would have been more useful to spend the time asking myself questions like: What are the ways I have benefited from being white? In what ways do I support and uphold a system that is structurally racist? How do my race, class and gender affect my perspective? There seemed to be many types of feminists and feminism. But instead of seeing these differences as divisive, I could have asked whether defining them was actually empowering and bringing about better understanding. But I didn't know to ask these questions.[10]

She has since acknowledged the problematic ideas she had about feminism, including thinking it is "easy" and "simple," which is hopeful because she is a role model, and the last thing we need is a generation of young women believing that calling yourself a "feminist" is the same as living your life as one. There is little that is "easy" about standing in opposition to a system of beliefs and laws that have existed for millennia and continue to have severe negative impacts on the lives of women and children around the world. Sometimes, we have to convince people that feminism can help us all be better and do better, and there are different ways to go about that.

Tina Fey is someone who has accepted the challenge and humorously brings her own brand of feminism to television and cinema. Fey is widely regarded as a funny woman with a CVS-receipt-length list of credits to prove it. From *30 Rock* to *Saturday Night Live*, Fey has left an indelible mark on modern comedy with her witty writing and often self-deprecating humor and demeanor. In 2011, she wrote an autobiography, *Bossy Pants*, and has since been referred to as a feminist icon.[11] I was a fan of hers from the beginning because I found her willingness to call out a lot of the nonsense in the world in effectively subversive ways refreshing and she did not seem to take herself too seriously. I would later realize, however, that she, like so many other White women with privilege, has a knack for going about feminism the wrong ways.

I first raised an eyebrow in 2013, when she and her regular partner in crime, Amy Poehler, had an exchange with Neil Patrick Harris, host of the sixty-fifth annual Emmy Awards. Harris was encouraged by comediennes Fey and Poehler to take his pants off and twerk. Harris said, "I am not twerking. I'm not gonna do that. That would be degrading." Poehler then responded, "It might be degrading, but we would be de-grateful." I was so bothered by the exchange that I wrote a piece for *Salon* that rejected their assessment that twerking is degrading and provided a reflective history of twerking, calling for an end to jokes about twerking made by people with no real connection to the style of dance.[12]

Fey has a poor track record when it comes to sex-positivity, which is why that joke prickled me as it did, even though it was delivered by Poehler. Fey has suggested that jobs like being a stripper or sex worker are beneath us, as women; they are, in her opinion, jobs we don't have to do because we are better than that.[13] Knowing how she views strippers, many of whom are Black women who twerk as part of their routines, I cringed at how the joke took her condemnation of strippers from being a blanket statement to one that was racially coded. Not unlike Lily Allen, the British singer who made an entire video where she featured Black women twerking (for the allegedly feminist 2014 song "It's Hard Out Here for a Bitch"), her lens lacks inclusivity and intersectionality. Fey does not seem to understand how calling an activity that women around the globe participate in degrading is harmful feminist practice, and she has been rightfully called to task by not only sex workers of all races, but feminist women of color. Women of color have been systematically denied opportunities for career growth and economic success, so by working in jobs including exotic dancing, escort services, or other adult entertainment, whether reluctantly or by choice, they are making their way in what may be the best option for them in their circumstances. Can it feel degrading for some? Of course. Any job can feel degrading if you are interacting with awful people who treat you like crap or if you are forced to act in ways you don't like in order to maintain your income. In the wake of the #MeToo movement, we see just how far and wide degradation spreads for even the wealthiest women, so why the focus on strippers?

It is not that we shouldn't extend grace to her and others who eventually see the error of their ways and reject their past commentary as narrow-minded or shortsighted, but Fey has often responded to criticism of her feminism by throwing her hands up, saying she isn't a perfect feminist, and moving along with little more than a shrug. No one is a "perfect feminist," but if you say you are a feminist, it is helpful if you actually understand that feminism exists to oppose hegemonic masculinity, and even better if you understand that sex work is one real way women can subvert the status quo and reclaim their economic and bodily control and power. We are well aware of how men have dominated and controlled the sex industry to the tune of billions of dollars annually, so why not critique their control instead of the women who participate in it as a means of earning a living? And suggesting that sex work and stripping is something anyone can rise above is a fundamentally patriarchal way of thinking that demeans women for being proactive in their own sexual behavior—hardly an acceptable point of view for an intelligent feminist woman.

It took a few years (and a growing online call-out culture) for Fey to reach a point of publicly acknowledging her fuckups when it comes to race issues. After the activist Heather Heyer was killed during a riot sparked by White supremacists in Charlottesville, Virginia, Fey made a joke that the best way to avoid Nazis is to stay home and eat sheet cake. I . . . I gave up.

A White woman was killed while actively fighting against actual Nazis, as part of the ongoing Black Lives Matter movement, and Fey's solution was to stay home and eat cake. She apologized for her bit and said she should have ended it in a different, less offensive way.[14] That is the aspect of White Feminism that is most troubling. These women do not often even consider the harm of their words and actions on people of color because they have no lens that helps them see how our existence and experiences are not like theirs. While they take an "all women" approach, one that *should* be the right way to go about feminism, it manifests in a dangerous "colorblind" orientation whereby they do not actually *see* how color, or race, affects our lives as women until they are called out or forced to see it. Campaigns like Mikki Kendall's #SolidarityIsForWhiteWomen exist in the tradition of women like Sojourner Truth and Amy Garvey, who made it a point to call into question the women's rights movements led by White women that excluded Black women by way of not including us as being worthy of advocacy. Fey suggesting that the way to combat racism is to stay home and eat cake was a complete slap in the face to every Black woman who has ever faced police brutality or suffered at the hands of White supremacists. If she was a feminist who was really about *all* women, she would have considered the history of Black women's experiences with racial oppression and might have offered better advice or at least not made light of what has been a long-standing problem in our country.

Racism continues to be the biggest threat to the efficacy of White Feminism™. Whereas Black men often struggle with accepting that sexism is as detrimental to society as racism, White women struggle with accepting that racism is as detrimental to society as sexism. Neither group is able to relate to what life is like at the intersections of race and gender, so they prioritize the oppression they experience directly as a result of their identity. The tension between feminism and Black liberation, at least in America, goes far back to the mid-nineteenth century when liberal White women were actively working as antislavery abolitionists. Initially, they worked alongside abolitionist men in the fight to emancipate enslaved Black people and end slavery for good. Once emancipation became law and Black people were legally freed from bondage, tensions between White men and Black women grew.

Elaine Weiss, an award-winning journalist whose body of work includes a significant focus on early women's rights activism in America, elaborates on how racism almost deterred the suffrage movement. In her book *This Woman's Hour: The Great Fight to Win the Vote*, she explains how, when Black people were freed, the women involved in the abolitionist movement called for everyone, regardless of race, to be granted the right to vote. The problem was that there were men in the movement who did not believe that women should get the vote, and prioritized Black male suffrage. As the women began to feel disenfranchised from the work, racial resentment grew and it was directed toward Black men, primarily. In the South, White men understood that, even if Black men won their voting rights, there were other methods of disenfranchisement to keep them from the polls (poll taxes, lynching, etc.). Women were another matter. Giving women the right to vote would weaken the powerful hold White men had on elections. Advocating against women's suffrage would preserve White male supremacy.[15] Couple this with lingering resentment on the part of White women against Black women, who, during slavery, were often forced into sexual servitude to White men, White women of the time found themselves feeling isolated in their fight for freedom and focused more on themselves.

Because of pervasive racism during Reconstruction, Black women became a liability to the women's suffrage movement. Giving *all* women the right to vote meant giving *Black* women the right to vote; in excluding Black women, White women had a better chance of success in pleading their case to a White-male-dominated US government. Even then, Black women as a prospective voting bloc were a threat to any candidate they would oppose as a collective, particularly in the South. We know that representation of Black people in the census would have skewed political power in favor of southern states, which is why, prior to 1865, Black people were counted as only three-fifths of a person—that is, three of every five Black people were counted as part of the population. Traditionally, Black people have heavily populated the southern United States, and with Black women's life expectancy during the early 1900s being longer than that of Black men, they stood to have a strong impact on elections.[16] As Sojourner Truth noted in 1867, preventing Black women from being able to vote while granting the right to Black men would only feed sexism among Black people:

> There is a great stir about colored men getting their rights, but not a word about the colored women; and if colored men get their rights, and not colored women theirs, you see the colored men will be masters over the women, and it will be just as bad as it was before. So I am for keeping the thing going while things are stirring; because if we wait till it is still, it will take a great while to get it going again.[17]

The impact of Black women has been significant since they gained the right to vote, and continues today. White feminists have only recently begun to tangibly embrace Black women's contributions to American politics, as the power of our voting bloc has become impossible to ignore (see chapter 8). In the 1970s, when the Feminist Party nominated Shirley Chisholm as the Democratic Party's candidate for the presidency, Chisholm herself said she faced more challenges being a woman than being Black. While Chisholm should have gotten support from political heavyweights like Jesse Jackson and Julian Bond, they opted instead to support her White male opponent, George McGovern, for the nomination. The division among women only added insult to injury, particularly when Gloria Steinem endorsed McGovern as well. What could have been a perfect opportunity for prominent, mainstream White feminists to be on the right side of history was lost when they did not show up for Chisholm, further hurting her chances for success.[18]

Social media has played a huge role in the increased awareness of intersectionality among White feminist women. Many have been, for the first time, exposed to intersectionality as feminist praxis by way of women like me, Trudy @TheTrudz, Mikki Kendall, Imani Gandy, and Kimberlé Crenshaw herself, who first introduced the term. Many have made it clear that they have had little education about other types of feminism, from sex-positive to Black Feminism. More and more, White women are showing themselves to be open to engaging in critical discourse that challenges so much of what they have long accepted and understood about their own identities and roles in the feminist movement. And they are crediting women of color who, for the most part, have little direct connection to the academy or any financially supportive institution; the way knowledge is shared via social media is revolutionary in that it increases accessibility and amplifies voices that might not otherwise be heard because of said "legitimacy."

When Donald Trump was elected president, White women tried—they *really tried*—to get it right this time, and came up with "safety pin feminism," an effort to show solidarity with those targeted by Trump during his campaign (LGBTQ people, people of color, immigrants, Muslim Americans, and many others). They agreed to wear safety pins to let these marginalized people know that they were "safe" with them.[19] Sigh.

Y'all.

*Y'ALL!!*

In response to this nonsense, feminist organizer Leslie McFadden created Safety Pin Box, an effort to educate White women in how to be more intersectional feminists and "allies." The idea was that White women would pay for a subscription service (Safety Pin Box), and each month they would receive tools that would help them do better: books, assignments, and swag.[20] The money generated would go directly to Black women. The idea quickly spread and White women around the country were participating in a collective effort to be better intersectional feminists. Instead of being educated for free simply by following Black feminists on Twitter, subscribers had to "do the work," and they were given tasks to participate in during their regular routines. They convened for Twitter chats and formed a Facebook group to keep discussions going about what they were being asked to do and what they were learning. The organization employed Black women and made regular contributions directly to individual Black women in need of assistance as well as organizations and efforts that centered Black women. It was a brilliant idea and, for as long as it existed, Safety Pin Box had an incredible impact not only on the lives of the women who received donations but on the participants, many of whom had never been involved in this type of educational endeavor.

This is an incredibly important shift in consciousness and one that cannot be understated: centering the voices of the disenfranchised and providing tangible support for the work being done and education being provided is becoming an understood and accepted way of making up for centuries of silencing and erasure. White women must be demonstrably involved in this shift, continuing to challenge their paradigms, expand their feminist praxis to reflect intersectionality, and leverage their privileges to make sure no woman is excluded from the fruits of the women's liberation movement. And just as social media creates space for these challenges to happen publicly, it also creates a community of women connecting across space and race and class to work on the issues that threaten to separate us, so that we can come together as an effective force in the fight to liberate *all* women.

CHAPTER 10

# Mammy 2.0

## Black Women Will Not Save You, So Stop Asking

*Being considered a leader can be a hassle. Some people put you on a pedestal and do not let you be human. It's like they see themselves in you—they see their best self in you and they expect perfection from their best self. When you're in that position, you want to live up to it. You don't want to slip or do the wrong thing. You're forced into feeling you should be perfect. That's not a comfortable thing.*

—QUEEN LATIFAH[1]

**T**HE YEAR WAS 2016. Two rich, older White people were running to be president of the United States. The American people had to choose a side and decide which one would be the best to lead the populace. On one side, you had the first woman nominated by one of the two dominant political parties, former First Lady, former New York senator, and former secretary of state Hillary Rodham Clinton. A longtime politician and advocate for women and girls, her career was marred by a philandering husband and her advocacy and implementation of America's imperialist intentions. On the other side, you had Donald J. Trump, a fucking fool. Ninety-four percent of voting Black women backed the woman. She was flawed, yes, but she was a politician, and when have we ever encountered a truly honest, *successful* politician? Despite accusations of past exhibits of racism and classism—not wholly unjustified—Clinton still garnered the support of the overwhelming majority of Black women voters. Many of us understood the importance of this election and, agreeing to hold her accountable for her promises going forward, we made the choice we felt was the best of the two. Eighty-seven percent of voting Black men backed her, too, along with two-thirds of all Latinx and Asian voters.

The fucking fool won.

Fast-forward to 2017 and everyone is a nigger.

In one of his stand-up routines, "We're All Niggers Now," comedian Katt Williams describes how everyone will begin to feel what "niggers" have experienced for centuries. His philosophy hearkens to that of Florynce Kennedy, who called out the government's "niggerizing techniques that are used [which] don't only damage black people, but they also damage women, gay people, ex-prison inmates, prostitutes, children, old people, handicapped people, Native Americans."[2] White people will get scared because they'll feel their safety is being threatened because of whatever political tide has turned. They'll feel like their rights are being limited and their access to resources being stripped away and denied. "We all niggers now. Oh, you did not hear about the 99 percent? It ain't about race. It ain't about White versus Black. It is about them versus us."[3] Though controversial, particularly given how some people use Blackness as a marker of struggle, his point was that at some point, non–Black people (Whites especially) will begin to feel something akin to what Black people in America have always experienced, and they will not know how to manage their own fears of being persecuted as they have persecuted others. And where do White people go when they're scared? Mammy.

"Mammy" is an archetype, a historical figure with unique characteristics and attributes. Donald Bogle, cinematic historian, discusses the development of the Mammy trope in cinema in his book *Toms, Coons, Mulattoes, Mammies, and Bucks.* Mammy first appeared in *Coon Town Suffragettes*, a 1914 blackface minstrel film, and then again in *Gone with the Wind*, that time featuring a real Black actress, Hattie McDaniel. Simply, a Mammy is a Black woman who takes care of White people's needs, from household domestic work to child rearing and family nurturing. She is always there, willing to cater to the needs of White households, often sacrificing her own health and well-being to be present for struggling White people.[4] The character of Miss Sofia in the film version of *The Color Purple*, for example, showed promise as a fierce, independent woman who fought back against domestic violence but was ultimately forced into the Mammy role by Miss Millie, the White woman who proved she could not function without Miss Sofia's assistance.

Mammy is often depicted as asexual/aromantic; she is not afforded the humanity of wanting or desiring love, affection, or partnership. Mammy loves her work and is always depicted as smiling and joyful, happy to be serving White people in their big, beautiful homes, which leaves little room for a personal life that might include being loved by a partner or even her own children. Mammy is often depicted as a larger, older woman with ample bosom that provides comfort and intimacy for needy White people, as her equally comforting fried chicken and collard greens await in the background. Mammy is wise—she has sage wisdom for every situation, and she doles it out with a pinch of tough love and a little bit of sass. Mammy is who White people turn to when they cannot figure out which way to go in life or when life simply gets too complicated and they need saving assistance.

Mammy was born during enslavement, when enslaved women had a life expectancy of thirty-three or thirty-four years. Hardly the sweet, less threatening asexual elderly woman portrayed in antebellum and Jim Crow mythology, Mammy was often raped due to her proximity to disgusting White men who felt entitled to everything she had to "offer." Mammy was expected to fix everything from broken dishes to broken White children. Mammy was often disrespected by her own people, especially by the men who saw her as a willing accomplice to White supremacy simply because of her intimate connection to White people, as she worked and often lived inside their homes. Mammy had scalded fingers, tattered clothing, physical and emotional scars, and never got enough sleep. Mammy did not have ready access to her own children, unless they, too, were working in or near the master's house. Mammy smiled through her pain because the laws long dictated that enslaved people were not allowed to express displeasure with their lot, so she smiled to survive and convinced everyone she was happy with her life.

Since 2016, Black women, vocal Black feminists in particular, have experienced the terrifying consequences of the reemergence of reliance upon Mammy, except this time, it manifests on social media platforms like Twitter and Facebook. When Black women took hold of social media platforms and used them to share their thoughts and have their voices heard, we were able to share stories and experiences that we'd long kept silent. We began writing, tweeting, making videos, podcasting, and blogging to express our thoughts about pretty much anything and everything. Much of this content centers our experiences as Black women, the good and the bad, the awesome and terrible. As White feminists (and others) committed to being more intersectional, they began sharing our stories, thoughts, and theories. And since most social media platforms function in ways that mimic the African conversational style of call-and-response, it makes sense that Black women would begin to dominate these spaces and utilize them in trendsetting and revolutionary ways.

We share our "sage wisdom." We organize. We create movements to rally support and generate resources to support one another. We make global connections, building community and extending our reach across continents. We produce and expand upon theoretical frameworks related to race, gender, economics, and politics in ways that are more accessible than most people have encountered; we make it easier to learn and understand the complex nuances of being Black women when Blackness is political and womanhood is perpetually regulated. We provide onlookers with new language to use so they can sound enlightened to their liberal friends and take on their bigoted coworkers. We challenge the way non-Black people think, speak, and act, and we encourage, and even demand, that they do "the work"—research, educate themselves, apply their newfound knowledge, and stop waiting for us to elevate their consciousness. We have called them out for their wrongs and continue to challenge them to better themselves, because we know if they don't, their behaviors will eventually be the catalyst for their own demise and we will likely be inadvertently impacted by their screwups and inevitably asked to be the clean-up women.

When Donald Trump was elected president, it seemed like people wanted to actually *listen* to Black women, at least when it came to social and political matters. All of a sudden, "Listen to Black women!!" became somewhat of a rallying cry for White liberals to appear "woke." Quite frankly, it was annoying at best and generally burdensome. Once again,

Black women were being charged with steering the ship under the guise of posthumous cosigning and appreciative support. What came off as "We're so sorry we did not listen to/value/acknowledge your contributions to . . . everything, but . . . !" felt more like "Save us, Mammy! Save. Us!" Rather than be honorably heralded for our brilliance, fortitude, and moxie, we became a frontline barrier to protect and guide those who were suddenly beginning to get an inkling sense of what it might be like to be subjected to perpetual oppression, or at least limitations on and boundaries around one's freedoms. What we do know is that when we are placed in such a position, we are also likely to take the blame when things do not work out as hoped.

The most annoying tweets have been the "Shut up and listen!" chastisement from liberal White women, especially, who want to think of themselves as "allies." There is more to freedom-fighting than retweeting popular Black feminist women on Twitter, particularly when their retweeting usually includes some type of additional Whitesplaining commentary. "I had to teach myself to just shut up and listen to Black women," they often say. Or they quote-tweet our clear, succinct tweets with a "Shut up and listen!! This Black woman is speaking!" addition that adds nothing at all, really. The problem was twofold, though. First, they did not just want to "shut up and listen," as they so often claimed, with White guilt-laden exasperation. They did not just want to learn from us and be "allies" in our centuries-old liberation fight. None of that was good enough because it did not serve their immediate needs or ease their new fears.

Second, many weren't willing to do "the work." When asked if they would refrain from attending Thanksgiving Dinner 2016 with their racist, Trump-voting family members . . . Crickets. When we needed them to be there to participate in marches and rallies against police brutality, they could not make the time, but when the 2017 Women's March was organized to take a stand against Trump, a president who represented the very same ideologies that led to police brutality rampantly increasing, they were ready to don pink pussyhats and sing "Kumbaya" over bongo beats.

They seek comfort. They seek salvation. They seek alleviation from the burden of truth and the challenge of real action. They want to ensure that Black women keep showing up in the ways that serve their best interests, so this new onslaught of admiration has felt less celebratory and more like pressure to add more work to our already full plates so that they, too, might benefit from our labor. They've begun to see us as Mammy 2.0, the perpetual supplier of digital comfort and salvation. They regarded us as wise (we are), they acknowledged us as strong (we can be), and they tried to position us as wells from which they could drink and be filled with refreshingly new points of view that made them feel better about being White (you cannot). They did not want us to be who we are; accepting the complex fullness of our humanity would mean having to respect our right to say no, which may have eventually denied them access to whatever comfort they were seeking in these trying times. They believed they were complimenting us by saying "Black women will save us," "Black women have been right all along," and "We need to follow the lead of Black women," but they were not. They began demanding more work without our consent, masking it as praise, admiration, and support, all while projecting their fears onto us. They were not so subtly asking us to come work for them and perhaps be their maids. As Miss Sofia tells Miss Millie in Alice Walker's *The Color Purple*, we find ourselves yelling back, "Heyull. Nawl!"

During this time, a number of longtime Black female politicians were garnering attention as they were becoming more vocal in their condemnation of the Trump presidency, both on television and social media. Women who have long been ignored or dismissed were beginning to gain clout as political authorities on all things Black and woman and liberal. Through social media, many people were being exposed to and learning more about Black women in politics and having to face their own embarrassment by being grossly unfamiliar with them until that point. Maxine Waters, for example, has been a representative in the US Congress, representing the Forty-Third District of California. Before her first election in 1990, she worked in California politics for fourteen years. This is what she does and who she is, yet so many were only then starting to actually *see* her. She's remained largely invisible to so many because of her race and gender, yet she has courageously fought and challenged rich old White men and their systems of oppression for decades. After Trump's election, she became more readily recognized as an internet meme used to add sass to tweets. Her facial expressions were hilarious, yes, and she definitely had some solid quotables, but the reliance on using her image to punctuate one's own liberal hot take was making me uncomfortable. People began to turn to her for guidance and leadership, suddenly putting their trust in her. She was being booked on all the cable news networks, and coverage of the work she'd already been doing increased, which was actually a good thing. Once again, we began to hear the refrain "We should have listened to Black women" in reference to underappreciated years of her work.

As you can imagine, Black feminists have been at the forefront of political discourse, action, and activism for years on social media. There have been so many brilliant Black women who have dominated this political space and have finally been getting the credit they've long deserved. Social media, again, has afforded these women space to share their thoughts and have their voices heard and, as a result, secure jobs and career-improving assignments and contracts. I feel a particular sense of honor for having the privilege to not only bear witness to their innovative approaches to political discourse, but to also know some of these women personally, either through collaborative campaigns, working together at conferences or on panels, or just spending sista-girl time with them at a potluck. I have joked a few times that one day people will look back at this period and be able to draw lines and make connections between Black feminist women on- and offline, and we will be seen as a game-changing cohort in the ways people look back at the writers and musicians of the Harlem Renaissance, the Combahee River Collective, and the women of the suffrage movement (minus the racism, classism, and ugly treatment of marginalized people).

Melissa Harris-Perry, a professor, award-winning author, and Black feminist comes to mind when thinking of how Black women have emerged as prominent political voices in media, both social and traditional. Though she is quite accomplished, many people, especially those outside of the academy, had never heard of Harris-Perry or her work prior to seeing her for two hours every Saturday and Sunday on MSNBC as host of *The Melissa Harris-Perry Show*, or *MHP*, from 2012 to 2016. Prior to getting her own show, Harris-Perry had several guest host opportunities and built up a strongly supportive fanbase on- and offline. A professor at Wake Forest University with a PhD in political science from Duke, Harris-Perry would commute back and forth from her home in North Carolina to New York City to record the show. A hardworking woman, she often shared parts of her personal life and presented as a solid example of how a woman can "have it all"—successful career, prestige, a loving partner, and beautiful children.

When Harris-Perry's show first aired, Black Twitter showed up and showed out to support her endeavor. Using the hashtag #Nerdland, users around the country tuned in to hear her takes on the latest news and engage her on the topics of the week. Her team used Twitter to share the syllabi for each show and asked viewers to weigh in on topics. Each weekend, we got two doses of her brand of political analysis with assists from some of the most important voices of our time. Harris-Perry welcomed everyone from professors and scholars to grassroots activists and unsung heroes, using her show as a platform to instigate critical discourse on issues that centered Black people, women, and most importantly Black women. Poet and mental health advocate Bassey Ikpi, Ferguson activists Johnetta Elzie and Cherrell Brown, and antipoverty advocate Tiana Gaines-Turner were among those given the opportunity to share their stories, elaborate on their passion projects and work, and connect with a broader audience that may have had little knowledge of their important contributions to social process otherwise. (I even made a brief appearance via video.) For the first time, a weekend cable news show shined a spotlight on the work and experiences of Black women, and many sistas felt seen and heard and finally represented.

For four years, Harris-Perry drew our attention in, making politics and economics more accessible and digestible, and encouraging us to challenge our assumptions and think more critically about what was going on in the world around us. She was not without controversy, though, and she faced a great deal of backlash for, among other things, being an outspoken Black woman who brazenly dared to speak her brilliant mind to millions. What #Nerdland taught me was how to be supportive of a sista even when I did not always agree with her; we can have differing opinions on topics and we can approach certain matters differently, but that does not mean I don't want the best for a sista out there trying to do what she loves and is passionate about. Her departure from MSNBC was not under the best of circumstances; Harris-Perry explained in an email to the #Nerdland staff after her departure that she felt she was being silenced and that she refused to be "a token, mammy, or little brown bobble head."[5] MSNBC had another take on what happened, but I'ma believe the Black woman, for real. There is nothing worse than feeling silenced when you are given a large enough platform to serve as a catalyst for important and necessary change. Her departure made way for another MSNBC regular, Joy-Ann Reid, to have her own show (#AMJoy) and, in many ways, pick up where Harris-Perry left off. Harris-Perry's audacious presence opened doors for many other Black women to permeate the rather White and definitely male twenty-four-hour news cycle. Yup. A Black feminist woman did that!

"Warrior" is the first word that comes to mind when I think about Imani Gandy, the fiercely brilliant lawyer, legal analyst, and advocate who challenges us to think critically about women as more than objects and incubators. I met Gandy through Elon James White, the brother who created the sex-positive weekly political podcast and network *This Week in Blackness* (*TWIB*) and whose contributions to podcasting changed the way many people actually *heard* the news and engaged in cultural discourse that centered politics. Gandy was his cohost for a few years, having grown a substantial following of her own through her blog, *Angry Black Lady Chronicles*.[6] Her subversive use of "angry Black woman" turned the stereotype on its head, and through her writing we understood that Black women have every right to be angry and more than a few reasons why we should be. I met her during that time, as I also cohosted a podcast on White's network, with the ever-dope N'Jailah Rhee, aka "Blasian Bytch." Gandy and I connected through *TWIB* and later at the 2014 political conference Netroots Nation, on a panel entitled "Black Feminism's New Wave" (with Chicago-based feminist writers Mikki Kendall and Jamie Nesbitt-Golden).

Gandy has long been a passionate advocate for women's rights, and she has a keen perspective when it comes to Black women's experiences with reproductive health. She quickly became my go-to expert on the latest legal developments in women's health matters; her sociopolitical framing of these key issues made them easier to understand and process, and her accessible writing made for easy sharing whenever I needed to debunk ashy conspiracy theories about Margaret Sanger and Planned Parenthood, for example.[7] Unafraid and unapologetic, Gandy battles the evil forces of sexism and misogynoir on Twitter almost daily, and she still manages to get in a few jokes and some of the best clapbacks online. Her political and legal podcasts reach thousands of people and continue to educate and move the needle on the most pressing issues of our time. As the senior legal analyst at Rewire, an online publication that reports primarily on women's rights issues, she expanded the publication's audience to people who had never heard of it before (read: me), and her contributions have helped grow its reputation as a trusted site for justice matters that deal with gender, race, and the economy.

If we want a great example of how being a vocal force on social media platforms can advance one's political career, Zerlina Maxwell is a woman who has come a long way and, if her growing momentum and support are any indication, has so much further to go. In 2012, when she was still in law school, the *New York Times* named Maxwell as a top political voice to follow on Twitter.[8] Much of the buzz around her was related to how she used her Twitter timeline to create conversations around political matters and weigh in as a new type of political pundit—someone who did not have to wait to be booked on a Sunday news show to share their political views. That is how I discovered her. I began following her online because I had not been exposed to many Black women who were occupying the political punditry space, much less being held in high regard as an important voice in politics. Maxwell's use of social media is a master class in how to establish oneself as an expert, build a brand, and use one's following and social media metrics to land amazing jobs and push one's career forward. She is an award-winning writer and activist, responsible for the notable social media campaign "#RapeCultureIsWhen," which encouraged people to share examples and identify the ways in which rape culture permeates our society and is perpetuated, particularly through media. As a result of the tremendous impact this movement had, Maxwell has become a highly sought-after public speaker on issues of campus sexual assault, rape culture, and feminism. And if all of that is not enough, Maxwell was tapped to be the director of progressive media for Hillary Clinton's 2016 presidential campaign. Maxwell's success is not simply about being on the right platform at the right time, as she is definitely an intelligent legal mind and hardworking woman. Still, she is a great example of how social media levels the playing field and allows for more voices to be heard and for more people to be seen, especially Black women who have for far too long been ignored and disregarded when it comes to politics. Like Gandy, she deals with her share of harassment and violence, vitriol and hate, but she presses on because her work is too important and her presence and representation in these spaces matters.

Meanwhile Black women have been identified as the strongest and most consistent voting bloc in the United States, yet we have not been successful in translating that political influence and power into political influence by way of holding key elected positions. In 2012, Black women's turnout at the polls was the highest of any group, and it was around that time that political analysts began to seriously take notice of the strength of our votes.[9] We rushed to the polls to reelect Barack Obama, yes, but it wasn't the first time we presented as an influential voting demographic. From 2012 to 2014, more than two million Black women became eligible to vote and added more to an already strong voting bloc, significantly increasing our political power in key nonpresidential races. As the numbers continue to grow, and Black women rally more support and strengthen our community, we amass more political power than many of us can comprehend.

What the 2016 election showed us is that Black women need a well-organized, impactful, and sustainable way to harness this political power and make it work for us. After centuries of performing free labor, prioritizing everyone over ourselves, the conversation has shifted to resentful discourse and the realization that for many, particularly on the left, we are only valuable as political mules, not necessarily as leaders. Enter Higher Heights for America, "the only national organization providing Black women with a political home exclusively dedicated to harnessing their power to elect Black women, influence elections and advance progressive policies."[10] Founded by Glynda Carr and Kimberly Allen-Peeler to support efforts to elect Black women in the United States and leverage the political power of Black women voters, Higher Heights for America and its associated political action committee (PAC) are "galvanizing the collective political power of our members to help elect more Black women to public office at all levels."[11] Both Carr and Allen-Peeler have extensive experience in the political sphere, from serving as chief of staff to elected officials to political consulting, and they tapped into their personal and professional networks to bring together people who are committed to supporting efforts to get more Black women elected. The PAC offers memberships for annual fees as low as $25 per year, making participation in political action more accessible to more people, especially lower-income Black women who too often feel disenfranchised from the political process and landscape. Through campaigns like #BlackWomen Vote and #BlackWomenLead, Higher Heights leadership and members use social media to raise awareness about not only Black women around the country running for office, but other events and opportunities to become more civically engaged.

As a member of the Founders' Circle, I have been able to support the PAC from the beginning and when Carr calls, I come and offer my platform, voice, and support in any ways that I can. I have to be honest and share that for most of my adult life, I have been jaded and cynical about political activity in the United States. I cannot help but understand the resentment or apathy other marginalized people feel when we do not see ourselves sufficiently represented in government but are asked to continue participating and supporting a system that is stacked against us. Sure, I have participated in efforts like Rock the Vote and hip-hop mogul Diddy's "Vote or Die" campaign, because I fundamentally understand the importance of civic engagement and the power of voting. I deeply understand the reality of voter disenfranchisement and when it comes to voting for people I am not confident will represent my interests as a Black woman, it almost feels like casting my vote is an act of self-harm.

I also struggle with feeling complicit, in some ways, in perpetuating White Supremacy, which is woven into the fabric of our government as it currently exists, regardless of who holds an office. In the entire existence of the United States government, 115 Congresses as of mid-2018, only 153 Black people have held offices in either the House of Representatives or the Senate. And the 115th Congress had a record 51 Black members at its beginning, accounting for approximately one-third of *all* elected and appointed Black officials since 1870.[12] Ten senators. That's it. Ten senators have been Black, and I am supposed to feel confident that my people and I are being equally represented in the United States government? With a collective sigh, we trudge on, though, and continue to do what we can to participate until we can make significant enough changes in government structure that truly represents America's diversity. Higher Heights has been committed to playing an instrumental role in ensuring that the future of United States politics is Black and female.

I reached out to Carr and asked her to share some of her thoughts about the progress and success of Higher Heights, as well as her hopes for the future.

**FEMINISTA JONES:** In the last five years, what has been the most important work Higher Heights has done?

**GLYNDA CARR:** I'm very proud that Higher Heights has been able to become the political home for Black women, providing them with a unique space to be informed, tell their stories and take action to collectively harness our economic and electoral power from the voting booth to elected office. We have also created a space for Black women who are running—or interested in running—to talk about and address issues that are unique to their candidacies and leadership.

**FJ:** How did "#BlackWomenLead" come to be?

**GC:** We created the hashtag in 2013. We were looking for something that would identify the full scope of our work and also uplift Black women's leadership. When we landed on #BlackWomenLead, we immediately felt that it encapsulated Black women's leadership on many levels. It's an affirmation of the unacknowledged work that we have been doing for centuries to move this country to Higher Heights. It's a descriptive, powerful statement. [In December 2017, Jeff Yang (@originalspin), political pundit and CNN contributor, decided to be helpful and support Black women candidates running for office. He thought he had come up with a brilliant and innovative idea: create a list of all of the Black women running for elected office and make it available for everyone who was interested in learning more about their platforms and how to support them in their races. He even encouraged the Democratic political action group Act Blue, to join in and support his groundbreaking idea: #BlackWomenLead. Oh . . . word? I cracked my knuckles and proceeded to educate him on the work of Higher Heights for America. Several others also let him know that he was co-opting the work already being done, but while he acknowledged our tweets to him, he did not stop with his rally cry.[13]]

**FJ:** After the hashtag was almost co-opted by someone who was not a Black woman, what have been the responses/outcomes? Did it hurt or help the brand?

**GC:** I don't think it's a secret that some of the folks doing this work day in and day out were concerned about it possibly being co-opted. This was right on the heels of #MeToo, and so there was rightly heightened sensitivity. That said, the experience functioned as an important moment for us. We were able to turn a potential problem into an opportunity to cultivate a relationship with an ally who had good intentions but wasn't aware that there are already groups out here doing the work. It served as a teachable moment. We saw our longtime supporters stand tall and proud as they boldly proclaimed that #BlackWomenLead had been leading in this space. It was truly an amazing moment to see the impact of our work. In this case, the man who used the hashtag reached out and became a member, partner, and supporter of our work. It reinforced for us that there are people out there listening to our message and wanting to support Black women's leadership, but they may be uncertain how to do it. These folks are genuine and more interested in building with us than co-opting our work.

As Black women continue to lead and as our influence in politics, culture, and activism is more widely acknowledged, one drawback I've observed and experienced myself is the increasing "mammification" of hypervisible, prominent Black women "thought leaders." I have seen people project their fears, needs, insecurities, and pain onto women who never asked or agreed to provide any type of engagement along those lines. I have witnessed brilliant women share their thoughts for free or for less than what White men get paid to be mediocre and have people demand they do even more. I have watched people beg and plead for help without so much as a respectful "Good morning, how are you?" or a basic introduction and exchange of pleasantries. People have, rather easily, reverted back to ignoring our humanity and relegating us to servants of their needs.

And it is not just White people who do it. Black women can expect that anyone of any race or gender identity will turn to them to be saved, to be fixed, to be "made better." The sociopolitical climate is such that people are frazzled and frustrated and do not know their ups from their downs, but they do know one thing that society taught them—Black women can fix it! Everyone feels entitled to us in one way or another, and social media platforms merely facilitate this abusive relationship in ways we probably did not imagine would happen. Perhaps our naïveté is partially our fault when history has clearly shown that society deems us unworthy of humanity and dignity. Why we expected better in the digital age, I do not know. So here we are, doing what we can to hold on to each other and lift each other up, and maybe, one day soon, we will learn to be more like Miss Sofia and Maxine Waters and "reclaim our time" when Miss Millie & Co. come begging to be saved.

Again.

CHAPTER 11

# Combahee Lives

*That's the reason why they try to keep women separated is because we educate and empower each other when we're together.*

—ROXANNE SHANTÉ, the Godmother of Hip-Hop[1]


**W**ITH THE RESURGENCE OF (at least a new, robust interest in) Black Feminism, particularly in discussions around representation in the broader feminist movements and pushback against misogyny within Black communities, more women are "coming out" as Black feminists (or "womanists," an earlier, alternative label embraced by many). Of course, there has been resistance to the growing movement. I think it is important, however, not to lose our connection to those who came before us and laid the groundwork for the work we do today. One of the most important trailblazers is the Combahee River Collective.

The Combahee River Collective was a group of Black feminists active in the 1970s. It was named for a military raid, the Combahee River Raid, planned and led by Harriet Tubman on June 1–2, 1863. She was credited as the only woman to have led such a raid.[2] The collective wanted to honor that legacy. The women sought to expand the National Black Feminist Organization to Boston, where they were located, and that was how the collective came to be. The NBFO was founded by Florynce Kennedy in 1973, the same radical Black feminist who created the Feminist Party (which endorsed Shirley Chisholm as the Democratic nominee for president in 1972), and the organization focused heavily on reproductive justice and rights. Among the members were Audre Lorde, Barbara Smith,

Chirlane McCray, and Demita Frazier, Black feminist lesbians who organized several retreats between 1977 and 1980 and eventually the Combahee River Collective. This vital work prepared us by crafting a blueprint for Black feminist organizing in the twenty-first century, and my own feminist praxis would be lacking without internalizing and embracing the collective's brilliance and guidance.

As the collective gathered, there were other brilliant Black feminist women building movements, gathering together, and publishing works representative of Black women's lives in the United States and across the world.[3] The Third World Alliance produced *Black Woman's Manifesto* in 1970, asserting, "The black woman is demanding a new set of female definitions and a recognition of herself as a citizen, companion and confidant, not a matriarchal villain or step stool baby-maker."[4] The Race Today Collective in Great Britain featured powerful voices like those of Leila Hassan Howe, and women like Althea Jones-Lecointe led the British Black Panthers in their work fighting anti-Black oppression in the UK. In Guyana, we saw the development of the Women's Revolutionary Socialist Movement, and in Brazil, Grupo Mulher Maravilha and Alzira Rufino's Casa de Cultura da Mulher Negra emerged as feminist collectives and spaces offering support for Black women. The period was ripe with revolutionary energy that changed the trajectory for Black women's global identity.

The women of Combahee drafted a powerful, cohesive statement, identifying their purpose and key issues for Black women at the time. It remains one of the most important documents in Black Feminism, and I am sharing some excerpts, with the hope of not only continuing the tradition of their work, but also of inspiring younger women or those new to Black feminist theory and practice:

> Black feminists often talk about their feelings of craziness before becoming conscious of the concepts of sexual politics, patriarchal rule, and most importantly, feminism, the political analysis and practice that we women use to struggle against our oppression. The fact that racial politics and indeed racism are pervasive factors in our lives did not allow us, and still does not allow most Black women, to look more deeply into our

own experiences and, from that sharing and growing consciousness, to build a politics that will change our lives and inevitably end our oppression. Our development must also be tied to the contemporary economic and political position of Black people.[5]

For the most part, Black womanhood, as a lived experience, relies heavily on accepting that there are two strikes against us, being Black and being women. And while many of us are taught at young ages that we will spend most of our lives fighting handicapped by the intersection of these identities, I argue that we must shift from a deficit perspective and begin to embrace Black womanhood as a powerful tool in our collective progress. When Black women win, we all win, so focusing our efforts on improving the socioeconomic conditions and political standing of Black women around the world is essential to our liberation as a people.

Above all else, Our politics initially sprang from the shared belief that Black women are inherently valuable, that our liberation is a necessity not as an adjunct to somebody else's but because of our need as human persons for autonomy.

Basically, if you ain't about that Black woman life, we ain't here for you.

We believe that sexual politics under patriarchy is as pervasive in Black women's lives as are the politics of class and race. We also often find it difficult to separate race from class from sex oppression because in our lives they are most often experienced simultaneously. We know that there is such a thing as racial-sexual oppression which is neither solely racial nor solely sexual, e.g., the history of rape of Black women by white men as a weapon of political repression.

I am very much invested in centering how Black women heal from sexual trauma by way of our art and how we reclaim ownership of our bodies through media like music. A lot of my recent work has been examining Black womanhood in music and how Black women employ musical artistry as a vehicle of not only self-expression but self-determination and progressive healing. Creating space for those who have been victimized to see themselves and their experiences represented in these public displays is powerful, and the universality of music means the message spreads far and wide, ending our silence.

When Black women sing or rap about sex, it carries more weight than when White women do the same. Yes, White women have indeed experienced restrictions on their sexual expression, and it is one area in which solidarity across races is vital. The racialized component of Black women's sexual trauma makes for deeper meaning when it is reclaimed in such hyperbolic ways. But the backlash against artists like Lil' Kim or Beyoncé, who, while markedly different in their music styles, have each embraced their sexuality and sexual identities as essential to their experiences as Black women, informs us of the discomfort felt by so many who struggle with witnessing Black women being so in control of their own bodies. Further, the denial of Missy Elliott—one of the most inventive, exciting, and influential musicians of the 2000s—as a sexual being because she presents her sexual self in a larger body is yet another rejection of Black women's sexual agency. Considering the majority of Black women, in the US at least, are overweight, erasing the validity of a larger woman's explicit sexual expression is a rejection of the majority of Black women's sexual identities. It's Mammification all over again.

When internalized, admonishments, borne of religious dogma and guidelines for chastity, only serve to deny Black women further control of their bodies and punctuate that denial with threats of eternal damnation just for fucking.

> We realize that the liberation of all oppressed peoples necessitates the destruction of the political-economic systems of capitalism and imperialism as well as patriarchy.

White male patriarchal supremacy is a plague and when Black men act in support of any form of patriarchal dominance, they are inevitably subscribing to the hierarchy constructed by the exultation of Whiteness. If

another brother says "Black men can't oppress Black women," I am going
to scream and cuss him clean the fuck out. Truth is, I'm tired.

> The psychological toll of being a Black woman and the difficulties this
> presents in reaching political consciousness and doing political work can
> never be underestimated. There is a very low value placed upon Black
> women's psyches in this society, which is both racist and sexist.

When we consider the obstacles to Black women's political success,
the attacks on our psyches must be part of the conversation. Not only are
we assumed to be incompetent leaders because we are both woman and
Black; we face nearly insurmountable odds when we simply try to engage
in political action and represent ourselves in the ways others are afforded
representation. White women and Black men continue to be severely underrepresented in political spheres because of their identities, so it should
be understood that existing at the intersection of womanhood and Blackness, two identities long persecuted for even attempting to participate as
equals in the political process, can lead to frequent assaults on one's psychological well-being. And it certainly does not help that when given the
choice of supporting a sista whose ideologies align with their own, both
White women and Black men have wretched histories of siding with the
opposing White candidate, citing winning odds and other such nonsense.
Perhaps if we rallied behind Black women more, their odds of winning
would be on par with their White or male opponents?

> The reaction of Black men to feminism has been notoriously negative.
> They are, of course, even more threatened than Black women by the
> possibility that Black feminists might organize around our own needs.
> They realize that they might not only lose valuable and hardworking
> allies in their struggles but that they might also be forced to change
> their habitually sexist ways of interacting with and oppressing Black
> women. Accusations that Black feminism divides the Black struggle are
> powerful deterrents to the growth of an autonomous Black women's
> movement.

As the young folks would say, "This is a READ," and as the aunties would say, "Oh, bitch . . .".

Listen, I am so completely fed up with the nonsensical antifeminist rhetoric that comes from some really ignorant Black men who absolutely refuse to relinquish the little bit of power-to-oppress they have as men to ensure that Black women are afforded our full rights as human beings. One of the most oppressive elements of antifeminist jibber-jabber is that it tries to force us into choosing one side or the other and that *force* is violence, totally disrupting their notion that Black men cannot oppress Black women. They attempt to forcefully erase the part of us they find most valuable, quite frankly, and it makes no sense to me. They want to use us for food, sex, and emotional support but also want us to deny the part of us they believe makes provision of those things possible. How does that work?

One of the arguments Black men make when they speak against feminism is that Black women have always been equal and that inequality and sexism did not come into our communities until Europeans did. That is straight-up bullshit, and perpetuating that myth is detrimental to our collective progress. Essentially, they suggest that sexism is a White thing and that there was no gender bias in Africa. Do these men even read? Study? Pay attention to anything that lives outside of their mamas' basements? While this pervasive myth is substantiated by claims of male African sociologists, there are those Black female scholars who work to debunk the myth and identify precolonial disparities.[6] The entire "Black Feminism was created to destroy the Black family/community" notion relies on an absolutism that an empowered woman equals a disempowered family or community, ultimately accepting that a woman's position should be inferior to a man's in order to maintain a strong family structure and community. And for men who believe their masculinity has been under constant attack by White supremacy, and that being leaders in their families and communities is the one way they can feel empowered as men, any ideology that positions women anywhere other than underneath or behind men is viewed as an assault.

Fortunately, a great deal of progress has been made since the statement was issued, in this regard. More and more brothers are coming into a more informed understanding of and appreciation for Black Feminism as an ideology. Many have studied it in their colleges and universities, some have connected the dots between the practical actions and words of the women in their families and the theoretical framework, and others have benefited from following some key feminist voices on social media and credit us for changing their worldview. I have had *so* many brothers tell me that I helped them better understand not only Black Feminism, but how women experience life on a daily basis. A lot of men are simply unaware of the challenges we face because we are women. They may understand sexism as a macro concept, but they do not give much consideration to gender-based microaggressions, because they do not have to endure them. Sometimes, it is helpful to compare our experiences as women to their experiences being Black—at least that starts the conversation. But they have to also be willing to accept that being *Black* women further muddles how we navigate the spaces in which we show up.

They also have to understand that when we point out the statistics about the violence Black women experience at the hands of Black men, it is not done to "bash" Black men, not exactly. We repeatedly make these points because

1. We are not usually believed when we share our individual stories, so data that validates our lived experiences can be effective;
2. Many Black men truly have no idea how much negativity we endure, because they are not directly involved in it, nor are the men with whom they closely associate;
3. We have been largely silent for generations, sacrificing our freedom and power as women to aid in the collective achievement of freedom and power for Black people as a whole.

We do not want to call the police on Black men when they are harming us. We do not want to live in the same fear of Black men that White women do. We do not want to send more Black men to jail, away from their families and communities. We have the lowest reporting rate when it comes to intimate-partner violence, while we have the highest rate of intraracial-partner violence.[7] It is clear that we have been prioritizing our families, our communities, and our men, too often to our own detriment, and to be accused of being race traitors and using feminism as a weapon to destroy the Black community—these are exceedingly offensive insults. Yet we press on and continue to try to use our platforms to educate as much as possible, believing that the more minds we can change, the more change we can spark for generations to come.

In 2014, when Imani Gandy, Mikki Kendall, Jamie Nesbitt-Golden, a Black feminist writer from Chicago, and I came together for a panel at the Netroots Nation conference in Detroit, "Black Feminism's New Wave," I knew we were onto something, especially since it was said to be the most popular panel and was standing-room only. I mean, they gave us one bottle of water to split between the four of us, but who was really counting? I immediately thought of how, in my various studies, I had discovered collectives of Black intellectuals and artists, people we have come to honor and revere. At the time they were coming together, I doubt they knew the history they would make and the impact they would have on Black culture. When W. E. B. Du Bois and Anna Julia Cooper traveled together doing Pan-African intellectual work, did they realize they would change the field of sociology forever? Did Stevie know having the Jackson 5 sing backup on a song would be as big a deal as it is for those who discover it for the first time these days? Did the Harlem Renaissance's "Niggerati" know and understand that their art and legacy would survive one hundred years, influencing innumerable artists around the world over generations?[8]

I began to think that we were our own sort of think tank or collective, and I knew I would want to continue working with these women over time. We specialize in different areas and our interests represent a broad spectrum of modern feminism and special interests—Gandy is a lawyer, Kendall is a military veteran who published a comic book, and I am a social worker who published a book on BDSM. I wanted to do more of these panels, centering our voices and celebrating our work on and offline, and, because of social media and the community we had all begun to build and participate in, those opportunities continue to pop up for us. I was never really interested in most panel discussions and conferences prior to becoming active on social media. Now I love not only participating in them, but attending them. The topics are interesting, and the proximity and access social media affords make me feel like I am going to see and listen to someone I kinda already know. And, to be honest, I just love gassing up women I call my friends and sistas. Whereas conferences have been historically skewed White and male, these days demands for inclusion and diversity (and the threat of being called out or "canceled" via social media dragging) have led to greater representation of women of color in these spaces. It is a wonderful feeling.

In early 2016, when Lemieux was still at Ebony.com, she and I did a panel together at my alma mater, the University of Pennsylvania, entitled "Talking Back: A Sex Positive Conversation About Black Female Sexuality."[9] When I found out I would be speaking with her, I was so excited, because not only do I have a great deal of respect for her talent and tenacity, I consider her a friend and colleague. We had a great conversation, and the room was full of supporters and people eager to listen to what we had to say and to meet us in person. She was the one to help me get my #Talk LikeSex column at Ebony.com, and she was a New York mama like me. Our discussion about sex and sexuality was like two girlfriends chatting it up over some bourbon and weed.

I've been able to collaborate at length with nearly every woman mentioned in this book, in some way or another, and it has been a dream come true to not only build community with Black women, but to be able to create space for us to share our stories and give testimonies that would live on for future generations to learn from and be inspired by. The pinnacle was the Women's Freedom Conference in 2015, an all-digital conference completely conceived and operated by and featuring women of color from five continents. In 2014, two friends of mine and I were having Thanksgiving dinner with our children and we began talking about hosting a rally or march of some sort to bring women of color together and amplify our stories. We would convene in Washington, DC, and invite women from around the country to join us for a day of solidarity building, speeches, panels, and networking. The more we thought about it, however, the more we considered accessibility to be an issue we needed to address.

One day in early 2015, I proposed to them we change the Women's Freedom *March* to the Women's Freedom *Conference* and have it be a day-long summit, completely online, that would invite participation from women around the world, who would not have to spend a dime to travel to, or worry about accessibility issues at, a physical venue. They agreed, and we set out to make history.

Serving as general director, I assembled an advisory board that included women such as Muslim activist Linda Sarsour, technology innovator Kathryn Finney, actress Reagan Gomez, disability activist Adrienne Gavish, and Lemieux, Hunter, and Elzie. Social media had previously connected me to all of these women, so I was able to reach out to them and every woman I asked was happy to support. We then put out a call for submissions and narrowed down our presenters to women of color who represented countries all over the world, from Kenya and the United Kingdom to Mexico and Australia, and included sports journalist Jemele Hill, Peabody Award–winning journalist Majora Carter, trans activist Lala Zannell, and social entrepreneur Tiffany Yu. The women, who were activists, journalists, artists, and entrepreneurs, represented every race and several ethnic groups from across five continents. It was truly a historic feat, with over forty women as speakers and panelists, and we pulled it off flawlessly, with sponsorship from SheKnows Media and digitalundivided. It was completely free and was made available in Mandarin, French, Spanish, and American Sign Language. With Lourdes Hunter as the keynote speaker at a live event held in New York City, we capped off an amazing event by centering a Black trans woman's voice, the icing on the cake.[10]

Combahee lives in the work of twenty-first-century Black feminists who bravely navigate the World Wide Web and streets around the world with a message of empowerment and liberation for Black women and girls. Their theorizing lives in Crenshaw's "intersectionality" and achieves clarity with Bailey's and @TheTrudz's "misogynoir." The radical work lives on in Gandy's reproductive justice and Kendall's "Hood Feminism." The spirit continues with Lemieux's narratives and Carr's political work, and it becomes visible in "girls" like Hunter, Cox, and Mock (i.e., #GirlsLikeUs). Their strength breathes life into everything we do, and it is a privilege to not only continue their work but to work alongside those who remain with us today and have their own presence online and beyond. Barbara Smith and Chirlane McCray are both active social media users and I am such a fangirl, it isn't even funny—what an honor it is to exist in the same space as these incredible women and even work alongside them as we push forward.

From Florynce to Imani, Marsha to Lourdes, Angela to Jamilah, Amy to Gugulethu, Audre to Sydette, Leila to Blair, Shirley to Glynda, and Anna Julia to Feminista, the narratives continue as does the work. The Mwasi Collective in Paris, a group of Black feminist activists whose Nyansapo Fest was threatened to be shut down by Paris's mayor because they said it was only for Black women and femmes, held their ground and reached out for support from us in America and sisters in South Africa. They raised hell online and we offered them what support they could. I only heard about it because it was organized, in part, by Fania Noelle, a sista who welcomed me into her home when I visited Paris and served as an advisor to the Women's Freedom Conference. The mayor backtracked and the festival went on as planned.[11] I love what the Bad & Boujee Collective is doing in Vienna, celebrating Black women's artistry and joy. The amazing Womanist Working Collective in Philadelphia, Pennsylvania is working to center the experiences of Black women and femmes. The Crunk Feminist Collective has been a stronghold for several years, founded by Brittany Cooper. The mighty Afro-Feminist Collective is fighting for Black women and against racism in Spain. There are more groups and they are getting younger and younger. Black women around the world are finding their voices and purposes and are using social media to build movements in the spaces they occupy. We are building a global community that is revolutionizing the way people fight for freedom, represent Blackness and womanhood, and influence media and culture. And it is only the beginning. With platforms like Twitter and Facebook connecting us and making the world between us that much smaller, we know that we will be able to accomplish so much more than Black women ever have been able to.

What's next?

One day my son, Garvey, and I were walking the streets of Harlem. He was telling me a story about something that happened in school and then he saw a man trying to "holla" at a woman. It was rainy and I was eager to get us to the nearest train station, but he stopped where he stood and launched into a bit of a rant. He went on, adamantly expressing thoughts about how unfairly girls are treated and how he couldn't understand why anyone would want to be mean to a girl. He said, "Mommy, we have to protect Black girls. . . . I know that. That's my job. Black girls matter, you know? You have my word I won't ever do anything like that to a girl. You taught me way better than that."

I have a pretty good idea of where we're headed, and I don't see us turning back.

# ACKNOWLEDGMENTS

My son, Garvey, is super dope. One day, he'll be a better writer than I am, and I'm excited for that. For the continued inspiration and motivation, I am eternally grateful to him for choosing me as a pathway to Earth.

Shout out to my editor Rakia Clark, who has been the most patient, kind, real, raw, amazing sista to ever work with on a project like this. Thank you for SEEing me and getting me to do this. What are we doing next?

Trudy, may the waves of the oceans and the whistles of the wind forever sing your praises. We can't "do this" today without you and I want people to know that, forever.

Yasssssss Factory, thank you for holding me down and lifting me up. Friendship is dope. Sisterhood is doper. Y'all the real MVPs.

Jeremy and George, your moral support has been so important. Love you guys.

Alex Millard, my assistant, who has held me down for years, through the ups and downs of this FJ journey. You are appreciated.

Julia Hudson, who made it so that I was citing and writing, writing and citing, in all the correct ways. I could never have completed this without you and your expertise. Thank you.

Dr. Meredith Clark, for giving us the language to speak about and the knowledge to understand it all. Thank you. You're the trailblazer here; I'm just walking in your steps.

Dr. Tracie Gilbert, for making the invisible visible, for inspiring, for listening, for sharing, for reflecting, and for making integrity sexy, thank you.

Mikki Kendall, Jamie Nesbitt-Golden, and Imani Gandy—the New Wave is here. Thank you for ushering it in and riding it with me.

Jamilah Lemieux, let no ashy-footed, crusty-eyed, YouTube University professor formed against you prosper. Thank you for committing to this work. It is an honor to work alongside you.

CaShawn Thompson, for sharing your story and allowing me to tell it. You are Magic. Thank you for the gift.

Dr. Herman Beavers, for always knowing the thing I didn't know and for pushing me to realize my own capacity and fulfill my promise. You may never know just how much I am in your debt and filled with gratitude.

Rachel James, D. A. Krolak, Freedom Side, Dream Defenders, and everyone who answered the #NMOS14 call. Thank you.

To my Twitter followers (at least the ones not regularly plotting my demise): your support over the years has been unequivocally the best part of engaging in any of this social media nonsense. When I'm down, you pick me up; when I'm out, you pull me in; when I'm cold, you warm me; and when I am ready to give it all up and walk away, one of you says the right thing at exactly the right time and it all makes sense.

To my Instagram followers, for always gassing me up: y'all make a sista feel good!

To everyone out there trying to make the world a better place not at the expense of others but for the good of all, I salute you, comrades, and appreciate your work. We're in this together!

To every editor and publisher who brought my words to life, you are appreciated. Wouldn't be here without you.

Prince, eye wish u heaven.

Leslie M., Shafiqah, Erika, L. Joy, Glynda, Zerlina, Bev, Tarana, Kimberlé, Cherrell, Chae, Jamilah, Adrienne, Angela, Sydette, Fania, Gugulethu, Dorothy C., Leslie J., Blair, Johnetta, Franchesca, June, Nyasha, Shevisia, Meredith, Vilissa, Tracie, Bree, Shafiqah, Evie, Kierna, Kathryn, N'Jaila, Lanae, Sil Lai, Natalie, Monique, Nnena, Olivia, Lourdes, Hannah, Zoé, Anthonia, Patrisse, Zahira, Chanda, Ivie, Kimberly, Shay, Janet, and every sista who has shared some part of her authentic self with me, supported me, collaborated with me, educated me, challenged me, dragged me, put me on, and gassed me up . . . I say your name and honor your truths. Let's meet at Combahee River and find ourselves in each other, affirm our commitment to our Truth, and liberate the world.

# NOTES

### INTRODUCTION: IT ALL STARTED WHEN...

1. @Cuba_Brown, "The weapon called Feminism that was a tool used to destroy the Black family and put Black men in Prison," Twitter.com, June 28, 2017, 1:26 a.m.

2. Quoted in Karen R. Good, "More Than a Lil Bit," *Vibe*, September 1997.

3. B. Drummond Ayres Jr., "Job Outlook Is Bleak for Vietnam Veterans," *New York Times*, June 5, 1971, www.nytimes.com/1971/06/05/archives/job-outlook-is -bleak-for-vietnam-veterans-vietnam-veterans-job.html.

4. Disaster Center, "New York Crime Rates 1960–2016," www.disastercenter .com/crime/nycrime.htm. New York City averaged 178,659 violent crimes a year during the decade of the 1980s; Dena Kleiman, "City Schools Open Today amid Budget Difficulties; Postponement on Civil Rights City Schools Opening as Officials Endeavor to Cope with Budget," *New York Times*, September 8, 1980, www.nytimes.com/1980/09/08/archives/city-schools-open-today-amid-budget -difficulties-postponement-on.html. New York City's severe budgetary constraints had a disparate impact on low-income schools and those populated primarily by Black and Latino students.

5. Maxwell Austensen et al., *State of New York City's Housing and Neighborhoods 2016 Focus: Poverty in New York City* (New York: NYU Furman Center, 2017), furmancenter.org/thestoop/entry/focus-on-poverty.

6. *The Prep School Negro*, dir. André Robert Lee, Point Made Films, 2012.

7. ΠΑΝΑΓΙΩΤΗΣ ΜΑΡΙΝΗΣ [Hercolano2], "Black Feminism, the CIA and Gloria Steinem," *Hercolano*, August 5, 2012, hercolano2.blogspot.com/2012/08 /black-feminism-cia-and-gloria-steinem.html.

8. Combahee River Collective, *The Combahee River Collective Statement: Black Feminist Organizing in the Seventies and Eighties* (Albany, NY: Kitchen Table/Women of Color Press, 1986), https://americanstudies.yale.edu/sites/default/files/files /Keyword%20Coalition_Readings.pdf.

9. Ibid.

### CHAPTER 1: #BLACKFEMINISM 101

1. Akasha (Gloria T.) Hull, Patricia Bell Scott, and Barbara Smith, eds., *All the Women Are White, All the Blacks Are Men, but Some of Us Are Brave* (New York: Feminist Press, 1982).

2. Angela Davis, "Reflections on the Black Woman's Role in the Community of Slaves," *Massachusetts Review* 13, no. 1/2 (1972): 84, jstor.org/stable/25088201.

3. Sojourner Truth, "Address to the First Meeting of the American Equal Rights Association," May 9, 1867, in *Society for the Study of American Women Writers*, n.d., lehigh.edu/~dek7/SSAWW/writTruthAddress.htm, accessed May 29, 2018.

4. Donna Langston, "Terrell, Mary Elizabeth Church (Mollie Church)," in *A to Z of American Women Leaders and Activists* (New York: Facts on File, 2002), 230.

5. Anna Julia Cooper, *A Voice from the South; By a Black Woman of the South* (Xenia, OH: Aldine Printing House, 1892), iii, available at Open Library, ia802702 .us.archive.org/25/items/voicefromsouth00coop/voicefromsouth00coop.pdf, accessed May 30, 2018.

6. Ibid., 31.

7. Ibid., 134.

8. Consideration also given here to Frederick Douglass, who was, in the same time period, making his way around the country (and the world) advocating for the abolition of slavery, and later, Ida B. Wells, the antilynching activist, who also made a name as an orator in the late nineteenth century.

9. W. E. B. Du Bois, among others.

10. The emergence of queerness at this time ushered in a new understanding of Black identity that has little documented evidence prior to the Renaissance. This isn't to say it didn't exist; we just have little evidence of Black queer identity as an open expression before this time. The risks of harm were already great enough for Black people without adding queerness into the mix. Blackness and womanhood were thus not the only identities intersecting to inform the experience of female artists.

11. Morgan Jerkins, "The Forgotten Work of Jessie Redmon Fauset," *New Yorker*, June 19, 2017, www.newyorker.com/books/page-turner/the-forgotten-work -of-jessie-redmon-fauset.

12. Mary Frances Berry explores the legal sanction of the sexual assault of Black women through the mid-twentieth century in her work *The Pig Farmer's Daughter and Other Tales of American Justice: Episodes of Racism and Sexism in the Courts from 1865 to the Present* (New York: Vintage, 2011).

13. Audre Lorde, "Poetry Is Not a Luxury," *Sister Outsider: Essays and Speeches* (New York: Crossing Press, 1984), 37.

14. "Voice" here is meant to represent all methods of communication and honors those who cannot use their literal voices or who find other means to communicate their ideas.

15. "End Patriarchy," *Ms.* blog, January 9, 2018, msmagazine.com/blog/2018/01 /09/end-patriarchy.

16. Meredith D. Clark, "To Tweet Our Own Cause: A Mixed-Methods Study of the Online Phenomenon 'Black Twitter,'" PhD diss., University of North Carolina, 2014.

17. Ibid., 7.

### CHAPTER 2: #BLACKFEMINISM 102

1. Lindsay Maharry, "Love Thyself: An Interview with New York Rap Queen Junglepussy," *KINDLAND*, May 11, 2016, www.thekindland.com/culture/love -thyself-an-interview-with-new-york-rap-queen-junglepussy-1455.

2. Rapsody and MC Lyte, "Rapsody & MC Lyte Discuss Being a Woman of Color in Hip-Hop & Their First Encounters with Racism in America," *Billboard*, February 1, 2016, www.billboard.com/articles/columns/hip-hop/6859468/black -history-month-rapsody-mc-lyte-interview.

3. @TheTrudz, "You have more followers than me? And you're a BW? That definitely means you you me service, Fact Portal mammy," Twitter, August 27, 2014, https://twitter.com/thetrudz/status/504745371570954241; Trudy @TheTrudz, "Black Women Online and Space Boundaries," *Gradient Lair*, May 11, 2015, www.gradientlair.com/post/113384203808/black-women-online-space-and -boundaries.

4. Mikki Kendall, "#SolidarityIsForWhiteWomen: Women of Color's Issue with Digital Feminism," *Guardian*, August 14, 2013, theguardian.com/comment isfree/2013/aug/14/solidarityisforwhitewomen-hashtag-feminism.

5. In 2013, the singer and so-called feminist icon Ani DiFranco announced she was planning a songwriting retreat to be held at Louisiana's Nottoway Plantation, a resort hotel that celebrates its history as an antebellum sugarcane estate whose enslaved Black people were a "willing workforce." Mallika Rao, "Ani DiFranco Is 'Remarkably Unapologetic' About Slave Plantation Retreat," *Huffington Post*, December 30, 2013, huffingtonpost.com/2013/12/30/ani-difranco-slave-plantation _n_4520487.html.

6. "Violence Against Women," World Health Organization, November 29, 2017, who.int/news-room/fact-sheets/detail/violence-against-women.

7. "Justice Dept.: Violence Against Women Fell 64% over Decade," CBS News, March 7, 2013, cbsnews.com/news/justice-dept-violence-against-women-fell-64 -over-decade.

8. @feministajones, "I'm with it! RT @BlackGirlDanger: @FeministaJones Can this be a thing? Can we, like, start a national #YouOKSis? Campaign?" Twitter, June 7, 2014, 2:37 p.m., twitter.com/FeministaJones/status/475391121510895616.

9. @miamckenzie, "LOL super late on this. I mean . . . not really. She came up with the phrase, all I said was 'can that be a hashtag for the summer' or something like that and then used the # before it. I didn't do any actual work and don't need any credit," Twitter, February 4, 2018, 8:57 a.m., twitter.com/miamckenzie/status /960195680693374976.

10. Sarah Koopman, "'#YouOkSis?—No, I'm Not,'" *Marie Claire South Africa*, March 5, 2015, marieclaire.co.za/hot-topics/youoksis.

11. Melissa Jeltsen, "We're Missing the Big Picture on Mass Shootings," *Huffington Post*, August 25, 2015, huffingtonpost.com/entry/mass-shootings-domestic -violence-women_us_55d3806ce4b07addcb44542a.

12. National Coalition Against Domestic Violence, "Statistics," ncadv.org /statistics, accessed May 31, 2018.

13. Feminista Jones, "Ray Rice: Black Women Struggle More with Domestic Abuse," *Time*, September 10, 2014, time.com/3313343/ray-rice-black-women -domestic-violence.

14. @bevgooden, "I tried to leave the house once after an abusive episode, and he blocked me. He slept in front of the door that entire night. #WhyIStayed," Twitter, September 8, 2014, 11:47 a.m., twitter.com/bevtgooden/status/509005057560707072; Nina Bahadur, "#WhyIStayed Stories Reveal Why Domestic Violence Survivors

Can't 'Just Leave,'" *Huffington Post*, September 9, 2014, huffingtonpost.com/2014/09 /09/whyistayed-twitter-domestic-violence_n_5790320.html.

15. Adrian Rapazzini and Mary Wilson, "New Again: Salt-N-Pepa," *Interview*, April 30, 2014, www.interviewmagazine.com/music/new-again-salt-n-pepa.

16. Jolie Lee, "#WhyIStayed: Powerful Stories of Domestic Violence," *USA Today*, September 10, 2014, usatoday.com/story/news/nation-now/2014/09/10/why -i-stayed-hashtag-twitter-ray-rice/15385027.

17. Pew reports that #BlackLivesMatter first appeared in July 2013, which is incorrect. Monica Anderson and Paul Hitlin, "3. The Hashtag #BlackLivesMatter Emerges: Social Activism on Twitter," Pew Research Center, August 15, 2016, pewinternet .org/2016/08/15/the-hashtag-blacklivesmatter-emerges-social-activism-on-twitter. This is part of a larger series by Anderson and Hitlin, "Social Media Conversations About Race: How Social Media Users See, Share and Discuss Race and the Rise of Hashtags like #BlackLivesMatter," Pew Research Center, August 15, 2016, pewinternet.org/2016/08/15/social-media-conversations-about-race.

18. @manthonyhunter, Twitter, August 20, 2012, 7:51 a.m., twitter.com /manthonyhunter/status/237562597128417281.

19. Anderson and Hitlin, "3. The Hashtag #BlackLivesMatter Emerges."

20. Movement for Black Lives, "Platform," 2016, policy.m4bl.org/platform, accessed May 31, 2018.

21. Johnetta Elzie, a native of Ferguson and one of the prominent figures in the Ferguson protests, was a founding member of this group, but is no longer affiliated with it. SaVonne Anderson, "Black Lives Matter Activist Johnetta Elzie Shines on New 'Essence' Cover," *Mashable*, January 6, 2016, mashable.com/2016/01/06 /essence-cover-johnetta-elzie/#1vrt_3cqViqb.

22. Brown went on to work directly with Kimberlé Crenshaw as community engagement director at the African American Policy Forum; AAPF, "Cherrell Brown," aapf.org/cherrell-brown, accessed May 31, 2018.

23. @susanmernitt, "Oakland local citizen media gets an F—review of the #*OscarGrant* coverage—http://snurl.com/9pe1z," Twitter, January 9, 2009, 12:33 p.m., twitter.com/susanmernit/status/1107598495.

24. Campaign Zero, "Planning Team," joincampaignzero.org/about, accessed May 31, 2018.

25. Britni Danielle, "Black Lives Matter Announces Leadership Change as Co-Founder Alicia Garza Announces New Initiative," *Essence*, February 7, 2018, essence.com/news/black-lives-matter-leadership-change.

26. More than a hundred articles were written about #NMOS14 and the events held around the US and in countries like Turkey and England.

27. Sandra Bland died in police custody on July 13, 2015, after having been arrested during a traffic stop and held in jail for three days. Her case made international news and rallied people in support. Her name is regularly mentioned in discussions about police brutality in America.

28. Andrea J. Ritchie, *Invisible No More: Police Violence Against Black Women and Women of Color* (Boston: Beacon Press, 2017).

29. Cheryl Corley, "'Invisible No More' Examines Police Violence Against Minority Women," NPR, November 5, 2017, npr.org/2017/11/05/561931899/invisible -no-more-examines-police-violence-against-minority-women.

30. Jennifer Scanlon, "Where Were the Women in the March on Washington?," *New Republic*, March 16, 2016, newrepublic.com/article/131587/women-march -washington.

31. "On the Masters' Sexual Abuse of Slaves: Selections from 19th- & 20th-Century Slave Narratives," in *The Making of African American Identity: Vol. 1, 1500–1865* (Research Triangle Park, NC: National Humanities Center, 2007), nationalhumanitiescenter.org/pds/maai/enslavement/text6/masterslavesexualabuse .pdf, accessed May 31, 2018.

32. I don't buy into the notion of being "emasculated" or "demasculated," because it accepts a baseline masculinity that can be altered in some way. I reject the notion of a standard code of masculinity, so I cannot embrace the idea that one's masculinity can be compromised by outside force in the ways described here. Much of the idea of being emasculated relies on homophobia and antiwoman sexism. Here, though, I use the term to communicate in a shared language so that the point is made clearly.

33. Connor Gaffey, "Bring Back Our Girls: A Brief History of What We Know About the Missing Chibok Women," *Newsweek*, April 14, 2017, newsweek.com /chibok-girls-boko-haram-583584.

34. "Chibok Girls: Many Abductees Dead, Says Journalist," BBC News, April 15, 2018, bbc.com/news/world-africa-43767490.

35. Quoted in Zeba Blay, "21 Hashtags That Changed the Way We Talk About Feminism," *Huffington Post*, March 21, 2016, huffingtonpost.com/entry/21-hashtags -that-changed-the-way-we-talk-about-feminism_us_56ec0978e4b084c6722000d1.

36. Ibid.

37. References #FeministSelfie, created by Black feminist Jamie Nesbitt-Golden, yet another hashtag/movement co-opted by White women without proper credit being given to the Black woman creator when the media covered the movement.

## CHAPTER 3: THREAD!

1. BlackPlanet.com launched September 1, 2001, as a social networking site targeting Blacks interested in dating, networking, job searches, and keeping up with popular culture, news, and politics.

2. Dr. Ashon T. Crawley, personal communication with author, n.d.

3. Lauren Dugan, "Twitter Basics: Why 140 Characters, and How to Write More," *Adweek*, November 11, 2011, adweek.com/digital/twitter-basics-why-140 -characters-and-how-to-write-more.

4. @FeministaJones, " . . . recovering," Twitter, May 17, 2009, 9:12 a.m., twitter.com/FeministaJones/status/1826743504.

5. Madison Malone Kircher, "Twitter's Secret Tweetstorm Feature Would Let You Plan Your Whole Thread Before Posting," *New York Magazine*, September 11, 2017, nymag.com/selectall/2017/09/twitter-has-secret-tweetstorm-feature-for -threading-tweets.html.

6. Casey Newton, "Twitter Officially Recognizes Tweetstorms with a New Threads Feature," *Verge*, December 12, 2017, theverge.com/2017/12/12/16754630 /twitter-threads-tweetstorms-feature.

7. Clarkisha Kent, "Hey White Allies? It Is Game Time," *Wear Your Voice*, August 16, 2017, wearyourvoicemag.com/identities/hey-white-allies-game-time; Savonne Anderson, "5 Initial Ways You Can Be an Ally to People of Color," *Mashable*, January 10, 2016, mashable.com/2016/01/10/ally-to-people-of-color /#ziKbkF9q3SqH.

8. Lauren M. Jackson, "We Need to Talk About Digital Blackface," *Teen Vogue*, August 2, 2017, teenvogue.com/story/digital-blackface-reaction-gifs. Jackson introduced this topic in her article "Memes and Misogynoir," *Awl*, August 28, 2014, theawl.com/2014/08/memes-and-misogynoir.

9. Ibid. The term "misogynoir" was coined by Moya Bailey; the theory behind the concept was developed by @TheTrudz to explain the unique type of misogyny directed against Black women. See Marie Solis, "Meet Moya Bailey, the Black Woman Who Created the Term 'Misogynoir,'" *Mic*, August 30, 2016, mic.com /articles/152965/meet-moya-bailey-the-black-woman-who-created-the-term -misogynoir#.VjW4CxnHf.

10. Ashlee Blackwell, emailed communication with author, April 7, 2018.

11. Jamie Broadnax, personal communication with author, n.d.

12. Jeff Bercovici, "Twitter Quantifies Impact of Live-Tweeting on TV Engagement," *Forbes*, September 18, 2014, forbes.com/sites/jeffbercovici/2014/09/18 /twitter-quantifies-impact-of-live-tweeting-on-tv-engagement/#7bc3d7a66ff5.

13. Matt Kapko, "How Live Tweeting Is Changing Broadcast Media," CIO .com, September 30, 2014, cio.com/article/2689318/social-media/how-live -tweeting-is-changing-broadcast-media.html.

## CHAPTER 4: THE INFLUENCERS

1. @NICKIMINAJ, ". . . Black women influence pop culture so much but are rarely rewarded for it," Twitter, July 21, 2015, 6:14 p.m., https://twitter.com /nickiminaj/status/623617003153035264?lang=en.

2. "What Is an Influencer?" Influencer Marketing Hub, influencermarketinghub .com/what-is-an-influencer, accessed April 1, 2018.

3. Feminista Jones, "Samaria Rice on Loving and Losing Her Son," Ebony.com, June 2, 2015, ebony.com/news-views/exclusive-samaria-rice-on-loving-and-losing -her-son-tamir-403.

4. Team Ebony, "Diversity of Thought," Ebony.com, March 28, 2014, ebony.com /news-views/diversity-of-thought#.UzW96_ldXP.

5. Transphobia: intense dislike of or prejudice against transsexual or transgender people.

6. Maggie Astor, "Violence Against Transgender People Is on the Rise, Advocates Say," *New York Times*, November 9, 2017, nytimes.com/2017/11/09/us /transgender-women-killed.html.

7. Janet Mock, "My Journey (So Far) with #GirlsLikeUs: Hoping for Sisterhood, Solidarity & Empowerment," Janetmock.com, May 28, 2012, janetmock.com/2012 /05/28/twitter-girlslikeus-campaign-for-trans-women.

8. Kendra Allen, "A Hidden Inequity: The Life Expectancy of Transgender Women of Color," *Consumer Health Foundation* blog, February 5, 2018, consumerhealthfdn.org /2018/02/05/hidden-inequity-life-expectancy-transgender-women-color.

9. "About TWOCC: Our Mission," Trans Women of Color Collective, twocc .us/about, accessed May 30, 2018.

10. We were working with limited funding and her honorarium was generally higher than what we were able to afford. Because she supported our mission, she agreed to do it and, one day, I hope to make it up to her.

### CHAPTER 5: TALK LIKE SEX

1. While at Ebony.com, I was able to write articles on Black female porn stars and interview people like Sinnamon Love and Mollena, two prominent Black women in porn and BDSM/kink spaces. I later wrote well-received independent articles on women like Lil' Kim and Missy Elliott, reflecting on their sexual energy and representation of Black women's sexuality in their music.

2. Adrienne Davis, "Don't Let Nobody Bother Yo' Principle: The Sexual Economy of American Slavery," in *Sister Circle: Black Women and Work*, ed. Sharon Harley (New Brunswick, NJ: Rutgers University Press, 2002), 103–27, law.wustl.edu /faculty_profiles/documents/davis/The%20Sexual%20Economy%20of%20 American%20Slavery.pdf.

3. Stacey Patton, "Who's Afraid of Black Sexuality?" *Chronicle of Higher Education*, December 12, 2012, chronicle.com/article/Whos-Afraid-of-Black/135960.

4. Dr. Tracie Gilbert, personal communication with author, May 24, 2018.

5. Feminista Jones, "From Slavery to Sexual Freedom," Ebony.com, October 23, 2013, ebony.com/love-relationships/talk-like-sex-from-slavery-to-sexual -freedom-777.

6. Feminista Jones, "Deconstructing 'Ho,'" Ebony.com, January 9, 2014, ebony .com/love-relationships/talk-like-sex-deconstructing-ho-333.

7. Feminista Jones, "I'm Not a Slut. I Just Love Having Sex," SheKnows.com, 2014, sheknows.com/community/love/im-not-slut-i-just-love-having-sex.

### CHAPTER 6: BLACK GIRLS ARE MAGIC

1. Ashley Iasimone, "Cardi B on Being a Feminist: 'Anything a Man Can Do, I Can Do,'" *Billboard*, February 12, 2018, www.billboard.com/articles/columns /hip-hop/8099087/cardi-b-feminist-stripping-interview-i-d-magazine.

2. Christopher Johnson, "God, the Black Man, and the Five Percenters," NPR, August 4, 2006, npr.org/templates/story/story.php?storyId=5614846.

3. Women are expected to cover their bodies 75 percent with clothing as Earth is covered 75 percent by water. As the Five-Percent Nation originated within the Nation of Islam, dress and dietary codes are quite similar to the codes of modesty adhered to by Muslims of various sects. For more information, see Ahmon J. Keiler-Bradshaw, "Voices of the Earth: A Phenomenological Study of Women in the Nation of Gods and Earths," master's thesis, Georgia State University, 2010, pdfs. semanticscholar.org/a9f8/efddb89c886a7fcdc5f612cbb2408aeba2f5.pdf.

4. George G. M. James, *Stolen Legacy: Greek Philosophy Is Stolen Egyptian Philosophy* (n.p.: CB Pub. & Design, 1954).

5. The blog *Very Smart Brothas* can be found at verysmartbrothas.theroot.com.

6. Linda Chavers, "Here's My Problem with #BlackGirlMagic," *Elle*, January 13, 2016, elle.com/life-love/a33180/why-i-dont-love-blackgirlmagic.

7. CaShawn Thompson, "Every Day Black Girl Magic," *Medium*, January 17, 2017, medium.com/@thepbg/a-long-long-time-ago-on-a-blog-far-far-away-i-once -wrote-about-what-black-girl-magic-means-to-me-c4642e4f2f96.

8. *Boy Bye*, dir. Chris Stokes, Footage Films, 2016.

9. Clover Hope, "Who Gets to Own 'Black Girl Magic'?" *Jezebel*, April 7, 2017, jezebel.com/who-gets-to-own-black-girl-magic-1793924053.

10. CaShawn Thompson, in discussion with the author, December 3, 2017.

### CHAPTER 7: TWENTY-FIRST-CENTURY NEGRO BEDWENCHES

1. Twitter Support, "About Online Abuse," help.twitter.com/en/ safety-and-security/cyber-bullying-and-online-abuse, accessed February 16, 2018.

2. bell hooks, *Ain't I a Woman: Black Women and Feminism* (New York: Routledge, 2015), 25–26.

3. W. E. B. Du Bois, *Darkwater: Voices from Within the Veil* (New York: Harcourt, Brace and Howe, 1920), Kindle ed.

4. Ibid., 181.

5. Kenny Anthony, "White Men and Fake Black Feminism: The Negro Bedwench Movement," Afrikan Library, September 7, 2017, afrikanlibrary.net/white -men-fake-black-feminism-the-negro-bedwench-movement.

6. Rodi Brown, "Cosplaying and Otherness," *Black Girl Nerds*, July 4, 2017, blackgirlnerds.com/cosplaying-and-otherness.

7. Shafiqah Hudson, "'Negro Bed Wench?' Negro, Please," Ebony.com, October 11, 2013, ebony.com/news-views/negro-bed-wench-negro-please-405.

8. *Late Night with Conan O'Brien*, season 13, episode 2129, air date October 12, 2005; "List of *Late Night with Conan O'Brien* Episodes (Season 13)," Wikipedia, en.wikipedia.org/wiki/List_of_Late_Night_with_Conan_O%27Brien_episodes _(season_13), accessed May 18, 2018.

9. Called *Hidden Colors*, the four-part series was released between 2011 and 2016.

10. Carl W. Kenney II, "Durham Resident Is the Author of the Willie Lynch Letter," *REV-elution*, March 21, 2013, rev-elution.blogspot.com/2013/03/durham -resident-is-author-of-willie.html.

11. Claire M. Renzetti and Vivian M. Larkin, "Economic Stress and Domestic Violence," VAWNet, September 2009, vawnet.org/material/economic-stress-and -domestic-violence.

12. YADA, "Menstrual Cycles Are Unnatural," Facebook, 2017, facebook.com /yadaawakening/videos/1926678307574189, accessed February 22, 2018.

13. Terrell Starr, "#YouOKSis? It's Time for Men to Be Proactive in Helping Women Fight Street Harassment," *NewsOne*, July 7, 2014, newsone.com/3033217 /youoksis-feminista-jones-street-harassment-notjusthello.

14. CRS [C. R. Sparrow], "Hotep Is the Modern Day A.B.S. and It Is Not OK," *Black Girl Nerds*, August 18, 2016, blackgirlnerds.com/hotep-b-s-time -not-ok.

15. Fee, "Birth of a Nation's Box Office Flop and the Unrepentant Pettiness of Black Feminists," *Medium*, October 9, 2016, medium.com/@inthe9thhouse/birth -of-a-nations-box-office-flop-and-the-unrepentant-pettiness-of-black-feminists -9f3f598819aa.

16. Vinson Cunningham, "The Birth of a Nation Is Not Worth Defending," *New Yorker*, October 10, 2016, newyorker.com/magazine/2016/10/10/the-birth-of-a-nation-isnt-worth-defending.

17. "Violence Against Black Women—Many Types, Far-Reaching Effects," Institute for Women's Policy Research, July 14, 2017, iwpr.org/violence-black-women-many-types-far-reaching-effects.

## CHAPTER 8: BLACK MAMAS MATTER

1. Mimi Abramovitz, *Regulating the Lives of Women: Social Welfare Policy from Colonial Times to the Present*, rev. ed. (New York: South End Press, 1996).

2. Dorothy Roberts, *Killing the Black Body: Race, Reproduction, and the Meaning of Liberty* (New York: Vintage, 1998).

3. Davis, "Reflections on the Black Woman's Role in the Community of Slaves."

4. Ibid.

5. Daniel P. Moynihan, *The Negro Family: The Case for National Action* (Washington, DC: Office of Policy Planning and Research, US Department of Labor, 1965).

6. Davis, "Reflections on the Black Woman's Role in the Community of Slaves."

7. Michelle Alexander, *The New Jim Crow: Mass Incarceration in the Age of Colorblindness* (New York: New Press, 2010).

8. Friends Committee on National Legislation, "Mass Incarceration and the Cycle of Poverty," May 2, 2017, fcnl.org/documents/335; National Conference of State Legislatures, *Teen Pregnancy Prevention*, March 2018, ncsl.org/research/health/teen-pregnancy-prevention.aspx.

9. Centers for Disease Control and Prevention, "Racial and Ethnic Differences in Breastfeeding Initiation and Duration, by State—National Immunization Survey, United States, 2004–2008, 2010," *Morbidity and Mortality Weekly Report*, March 26, 2010, cdc.gov/mmwr/preview/mmwrhtml/mm5911a2.htm#tab1.

10. Centers for Disease Control and Prevention, "Racial Disparities in Access to Maternity Care Practices That Support Breastfeeding —United States, 2011," *Morbidity and Mortality Weekly Report*, August 22, 2014, cdc.gov/mmwr/preview/mmwrhtml/mm6333a2.htm?s_cid=mm6333a2_w.

11. Ibid.

12. M. A. Crawford, A. S. Mendoza-Vasconez, and B. A. Larsen, "Type II Diabetes Disparities in Diverse Women: The Potential Roles of Body Composition, Diet, and Physical Activity," *Women's Health* 11, no. 6 (2015): 913–27, journals.sagepub.com/doi/pdf/10.2217/whe.15.62.

13. Black Women Do Breastfeed, blackwomendobreastfeed.org, accessed May 19, 2018.

14. Rob Haskell, "Serena Williams on Motherhood, Marriage, and Making Her Comeback," *Vogue*, January 10, 2018, vogue.com/article/serena-williams-vogue-cover-interview-february-2018.

15. Ibid.

16. Ibid.

17. Linda Villarosa, "Why America's Black Mothers and Babies Are in a Life-or-Death Crisis," *New York Times Magazine*, April 11, 2018, nytimes.com/2018/04/11/magazine/black-mothers-babies-death-maternal-mortality.html.

18. Centers for Disease Control and Prevention, "Pregnancy Mortality Surveillance System," November 9, 2017, cdc.gov/reproductivehealth/maternalinfant health/pmss.html.

19. Villarosa, "Why America's Black Mothers and Babies Are in a Life-or-Death Crisis."

20. Siobhan Fenton, "How Sexist Stereotypes Mean Doctors Ignore Women's Pain," *Independent*, July 27, 2016, independent.co.uk/life-style/health-and-families /health-news/how-sexist-stereotypes-mean-doctors-ignore-womens-pain-a7157931 .html.

21. Ibid.

22. Astha Singhal, Yu-Yu Tien, and Renee Y. Hsia, "Racial-Ethnic Disparities in Opioid Prescriptions at Emergency Department Visits for Conditions Commonly Associated with Prescription Drug Abuse," *PLoSOne* (August 8, 2016), journals.plos .org/plosone/article?id=10.1371%2Fjournal.pone.0159224.

23. Mater Mea, matermea.com, 2012.

24. The "Lean In" discourse followed from the book of the same title by Sheryl Sandberg, COO of Facebook; the book received both praise for its frank discussion of being a woman in a male-dominated industry, and criticism for Sandberg's apparent ignorance with regard to race, class, and even the gendered division of labor in the home. Sheryl Sandberg and Nell Scovell, *Lean In: Women, Work, and the Will to Lead* (New York: Alfred A. Knopf, 2013).

25. Anthonia Akitunde, personal communication with author, April 24, 2018.

26. "Our Story," BlackMomsConnection.com, blackmomsconnection.com /ourstory, accessed May 22, 2018.

27. Sarah Gonzalez and Jenny Ye, "Black Mothers Judged Unfit at Higher Rate than White Mothers in NJ," *WNYC News*, May 26, 2015, wnyc.org/story/black -parents-nj-lose-custody-their-kids-more-anyone-else.

28. American Academy of Pediatrics, Committee on Early Childhood, Adoption, and Dependent Care, "Developmental Issues for Young Children in Foster Care," *Pediatrics* 106, no. 5 (2000), pediatrics.aappublications.org/content/pediatrics /106/5/1145.full.pdf.

**CHAPTER 9: "I'VE ALWAYS BEEN GOOD TO YOU PEOPLE!"**

1. Amy Euphemia Jacques Garvey, "Women as Leaders," 1925, History Is a Weapon.com, historyisaweapon.com/defcon1/garveywomenasleaders.html, accessed May 24, 2018.

2. In using the trademark symbol here, I am referencing "White Feminism" as the often-flawed mainstream approach to feminism projected by White women whose feminism seems to primarily apply to them without much consideration for how their ideas may negatively affect women of color.

3. Andrea Chang and Ryan Faughnder, "No One Took Rose McGowan's Claims Seriously. Now Everyone Is Listening," *Los Angeles Times*, October 13, 2017, latimes.com/business/la-fi-rose-mcgowan-harvey-weinstein-20171013-story.html.

4. Ashley Louszko et al., "Rose McGowan Describes Alleged Rape by Harvey Weinstein, Her Thoughts on the Hollywood 'System,'" ABC News.com, January 30, 2018, abcnews.go.com/Entertainment/rose-mcgowan-describes-alleged-rape -harvey-weinstein-thoughts/story?id=52684109.

5. @chrissgardner, "Straight out gate, host @JKCorden with Harvey Weinstein jokes. Too soon? Some laughs, some groans #amfARLosAngeles," Twitter, October 13, 2017, 10:47 p.m., twitter.com/chrissgardner/status/919031962546847744.

6. @rosemcgowan, "THIS IS RICH FAMOUS HOLLYWOOD WHITE MALE PRIVILEGE IN ACTION. REPLACE THE WORD 'WOMEN' w/ the 'N' word, how does it feel?" Twitter, October 15, 2017, 7:34 a.m. The tweet has since been deleted.

7. Chang and Faughnder, "No One Took Rose McGowan's Claims Seriously."

8. HeForShe, "Our Mission," 2016, heforshe.org/en/our-mission, accessed May 28, 2018.

9. Nina Bradley, "Emma Watson Just Admitted to Being a 'White Feminist' & It's a Lesson in Self-Awareness," *Bustle*, April 24, 2018, bustle.com/p/emma-watsons -comments-on-white-feminism-are-a-lesson-in-self-awareness-intersectionality -7842357.

10. Emma Watson, "Announcements: First Book of 2018! *Why I'm No Longer Talking to White People About Race* by Reni Eddo-Lodge," "Our Shared Shelf," Goodreads.com, December 31, 2017, goodreads.com/topic/show/19152741-first -book-of-2018-why-i-m-no-longer-talking-to-white-people-about-race.

11. Martha Lauzen, "The Funny Business of Being Tina Fey: Constructing a (Feminist) Comedy Icon," *Feminist Media Studies* 14, no. 1 (2012): 106–17, doi:10.10 80/14680777.2012.740060.

12. Feminista Jones, "End Stupid Twerking Jokes Once and for All," *Salon*, September 24, 2013, salon.com/2013/09/24/end_stupid_twerking_jokes_once_and _for_all.

13. Maureen Dowd, "What Tina Fey Wants," *Vanity Fair*, December 1, 2008, vanityfair.com/culture/2009/01/tina-fey200901.

14. "Tina Fey Admits She 'Screwed Up' Charlottesville SNL Bit: 'I Wanted to Help and I Chumped It,'" *People*, March 4, 2018, people.com/tv/tina-fey-screwed-up-charlottesville-snl-bit.

15. Elaine Weiss, *The Woman's Hour: The Great Fight to Win the Vote* (New York: Viking, 2018).

16. National Center for Health Statistics, "Life Expectancy," 2016, "Table 15 (page 1 of 2). Life expectancy at birth, at age 65, and at age 75, by sex, race, and Hispanic origin: United States, selected years 1900–2015," Centers for Disease Control and Prevention, cdc.gov/nchs/data/hus/2016/015.pdf, accessed May 29, 2018.

17. Truth, "Address to the First Meeting of the American Equal Rights Association."

18. Jackson Landers, "'Unbought and Unbossed': When a Black Woman Ran for the White House," *Smithsonian*, April 25, 2016, smithsonianmag.com/smithsonian -institution/unbought-and-unbossed-when-black-woman-ran-for-the-white-house -180958699.

19. Landess Kearns, "The Incredible Reason You Might Start Seeing Safety Pins Everywhere," *Huffington Post*, November 11, 2016, www.huffingtonpost.com/entry /safety-pin-trump-brexit_us_58251b53e4b0c4b63b0c11a9.

20. "Safety Pin Box: White People Can Now Pay for Those 'How Not to Be Racist' Lessons," *Root*, January 12, 2017, www.theroot.com/safety-pin-box-white -people-can-now-pay-for-those-how-1790858201.

CHAPTER 10: MAMMY 2.0

1. Dennis Hunt, "10 Questions: Queen Latifah," *Los Angeles Times*, September 8, 1991, http://articles.latimes.com/1991-09-08/entertainment/ca-2712_1_queen -latifah.

2. Sherie Randolph, *Florynce "Flo" Kennedy: The Life of a Black Feminist Radical* (Chapel Hill: University of North Carolina Press, 2015).

3. *Kattpacalypse*, Marcus Raboy, dir., Kattpack Investments and Entertainment One, 2012. Clips found at cc.com/episodes/8myuhp/katt-williams—kattpacalypse -katt-williams—kattpacalypse-season-1-ep-101, accessed August 1, 2017.

4. Donald Bogle, *Toms, Coons, Mulattoes, Mammies, and Bucks: An Interpretive History of Blacks in American Films*, 3rd ed. (New York: Continuum International Publishing Group, 1994).

5. Jamil Smith, "Melissa Harris-Perry's Email to Her #Nerdland Staff," *Medium*, February 16, 2016, medium.com/@JamilSmith/melissa-harris-perry-s-email-to-her -nerdland-staff-11292bdc27cb.

6. Imani Gandy, "Angry Black Lady Chronicles," *Rewire News*, rewire.news/ablc, accessed May 22, 2018.

7. Imani Gandy, "How False Narratives of Margaret Sanger Are Being Used to Shame Black Women," *Rewire News*, August 20, 2015, rewire.news/article/2015 /08/20/false-narratives-margaret-sanger-used-shame-black-women.

8. Ben Smith, "A Twitter Voice to Follow," *New York Times*, July 10, 2012, thecaucus.blogs.nytimes.com/2012/07/10/a-twitter-voice-to-follow.

9. Maya Harris, "Women of Color: A Growing Force in the American Electorate," *American Progress*, October 30, 2014, americanprogress.org/issues/race/reports /2014/10/30/99962/women-of-color.

10. Higher Heights, "About," higherheightsforamerica.org/about_higher_heights, accessed May 18, 2018.

11. Ibid.

12. Ida A. Brudnick and Jennifer E. Manning, "African American Members of the United States Congress: 1870–2018," Congressional Research Service, April 26, 2018, senate.gov/CRSpubs/617f17bb-61e9-40bb-b301-50f48fd239fc.pdf.

13. @originalspin, "Hey guys, I cleaned up and will continue to grow this list of #BlackWomenLead candidates. Please share—and donate. @actblue—would love to talk about creating a 'lovebomb' system letting us give to everyone on this list with one click. #GiveBackGiveBlack," Twitter, December 13, 2017, 10:07 a.m., twitter.com/originalspin/status/941006737644982272.

CHAPTER 11: COMBAHEE LIVES

1. Breakfast Club, "Roxanne Shante Finally Gets Her Revenge, Talks Hip-Hop Queens & More," IHeart Radio, March 23, 2018, https://thebreakfastclub.iheart .com/featured/breakfast-club/content/2018-03-23-roxanne-shante-finally-gets-her -revenge-talks-hip-hop-queens-more/.

2. Barbara Maranzani, "Harriet Tubman's Daring Raid, 150 Years Ago," History .com, A&E Television Networks, May 31, 2013, www.history.com/news/harriet -tubmans-daring-raid-150-years-ago.

3. Kimberly Springer, "The Interstitial Politics of Black Feminist Organizations," *Meridians* 1, no. 2 (2001): 155–91, www.jstor.org/stable/40338461.

4. Third World Women's Alliance, *Black Woman's Manifesto* (New York: Third World Women's Alliance, 1970), https://library.duke.edu/digitalcollections/wlmpc _wlmms01009.

5. Combahee River Collective, *The Combahee River Collective Statement*.

6. Tola Olu Pearce, "Dispelling the Myth of Pre-Colonial Gender Equality in Yoruba Culture," *Canadian Journal of African Studies/Revue canadienne des études afric-aines* 48, no. 2 (February 6, 2015): 315–31, doi:10.1080/00083968.2014.951665.

7. Jones, "From Slavery to Sexual Freedom."

8. "Niggerati" refers to the publishers and writers of the journal *Fire*, pub-lished during the Harlem Renaissance, and other artists of the Black Bourgeoisie. The group, the name coined by Wallace Thurman, included Thurman, Langston Hughes, Zora Neale Hurston, Richard Wright, Claude McKay, and others.

9. "Talking Back: A Sex Positive Conversation About Black Female Sexuality," presented by BGAPSA, University of Pennsylvania, February 26, 2016.

10. Kaya Thomas, "Women's Freedom Conference Amplifies the Voices of Women of Color," *TechCrunch*, October 28, 2015, techcrunch.com/2015/10/28 /womens-freedom-conference-amplifies-the-voices-of-women-of-color.

11. Brenna Daldorph, "Paris Mayor Vows to Halt Black Feminist Festival, Then Backtracks," *France 24*, May 30, 2017, www.france24.com/en/20170529-paris-mayor -hidalgo-vows-ban-black-feminist-event.